GUIDEBOOK

YOUR GUIDE THROUGH
THE FLORIDA COLLEGE & UNIVERSITY SYSTEM

by

Dr. Amanda Sterk, Ed.D

the Peppertree Press

Sarasota, Florida

This *College UnMazed Guidebook* was a true passion of mine to meet the needs of students throughout Florida.

Without the loving support of my family, friends and colleagues this guidebook would not have been possible. Through the hundreds of hours of researching, writing, seeking clarification, discussing with experts, and organizing the information in an easy to read format that all parents and students could utilize, I was encouraged every step of the way.

Personal acknowledgements to:

My loving, extremely supportive husband, Heath, and beautiful daughters, Eden and Rilah. You three are my constant cheerleaders and motivators. I could not have done it without you.

My colleagues from all the wonderful schools I have been at. You have mentored and guided me to what great education looks like, especially Jeri Sanburn, Don Arends, Michele Richardson, and Dr. Brian Botts.

My Florida tribe of educational experts who answered all of my questions, and also believe in college and career readiness as much as I do. A special thank you to the FutureMakers Coalition, Dr. Rebecca Schumacher, Lori Brooks, and the many school counselors and admission representatives who work tirelessly for their students.

My wonderful students who I have had the privilege to be a part of their lives as they sought their college and career dreams. Their stories, their passion, and their uniqueness drive me every day to create better programming so they have every opportunity available to reach their lifelong goals.

For information regarding permission, call 941-922-2662 or contact us at our website: www.peppertreepublishing.com or write to: the Peppertree Press, LLC.

Attention: Publisher

1269 First Street, Suite 7

Sarasota, Florida 34236

ISBN: 978-1-61493-544-5

Library of Congress Number: 2017913304

Printed September 2017

Parent & Student Letter

Dear High School Students,

This is a great time for you! Whether you are a freshman just starting the process, or a senior looking at the next phase of life, this *College UnMazed: Your Guide Through the Florida College & University System* was created just for you as you embark on the next phase of your educational journey—COLLEGE! This should be a team effort, and the more you include your parents, educators, school counselor, college admissions representatives, those around you, and all of the UnMaze.Me resources, the better and easier this process will be.

I have created several resources for you to help guide you through this process. This *Guidebook* is to be used in conjunction with the resources I have created through the UnMaze.Me website, including the online courses, webinars, and articles. While it may seem like a lot all at once, if you make a plan to tackle things in smaller chunks, it will truly be so much easier and less time-consuming. Students who plan and prepare throughout the year end up with better admission decisions, more scholarship money, and a less stressful year with more college choices.

Use this book as your guide from freshman to your senior year, but also remember that I will be adding information frequently to all these social media resources:

www.unmaze.me

facebook/highschoolsimplied

@unmazeme

As always, I am here to be a resource and help for you.

Dr. Amanda Sterk

Founder of UnMaze Me

ENDORSEMENTS:

"Amanda not only cares and is passionate about helping students get to college, she also really knows her stuff!"

Julie, Parent

"Amanda is amazing. She truly is filling a need with her site and this guidebook. There is so much information out there and Amanda helps simplify it. She is truly knowledgeable and passionate about what she does. My daughter just finished up with her College UnMazed class in Cape Coral and I couldn't be happier. She has truly opened our eyes! Highly Highly Highly recommend!!!"

Kathleen, Parent

"Amanda has played a major role in guiding my eldest daughter through the difficult process of registering for college courses through dual-enrollment, and has also been very influential in guiding our daughter with the different Florida colleges and the many scholarships that are offered.

I can honestly say that Amanda has played a very large part in our daughters' lives this past year. We were very fortunate to find her. She has helped make our move here to the Cape a success and we could have never done this without her!"

Kristie, Parent

"This is guidebook is so exciting! You have done wonderful things for our school and now for our community. I am glad that you have written a book to help all high school students and parents out."

Tracey, Parent

"Dr. Sterk is passionate about guiding students through the college process. She continually seeks to collaborate with experts in the field and ensures the highest quality information is passed on to families that need it most. As a college and career counselor, I see how instrumental her College UnMazed Guidebook will be to ALL Florida students."

Nancy Frede, Find Your Future Today, Career Coach

FOREWORD

Children as young as five years to as old as 18 years **ALL** desire a future filled with success and security. Children want to grow up to be something. Just ask any first grader what they want to be and answers range from – Veterinarian, Engineer, Nurse, Police Officer, Doctor, Banker, Fireman, Lawyer...And my favorites - "Cowboy, Spiderman, Princess". One recent response from a first grader in particularly captured my heart -- "I'm going to be the next Martin Luther King".

EVERY child dreams and desires for an adult future of worth and success.

I spend a great deal of time in prek-12 schools to support the work of school counselors and guide graduate school counseling students in their professional development. Most of this work is related to developing a college-going culture, where I spend the majority of my time in schools where children are not fortunate to reside in neighborhoods of economic prosperity, and instead endure crime, drugs, gang violence, and poverty. I have many discussions with students about their futures, and I am consistently impressed with their aspirations and enthusiasm, and inspired to devote my time to college and career readiness. Many, if not **ALL** children, want and intend to go to college. Even the younger children often aspire to enroll in a specific college because they like the school colors, the school mascot, or the football team. Ultimately though, high school seniors make college decisions and submit applications based on a host of reasons. If only this process was as simple as choosing a mascot, color, or team, yet we know there are complexities involved with this process.

Regardless of family structure, zip code, ethnicity, race, economic status – we know that every child needs support and guidance to find the pathway to a prosperous life. Some families, particularly those who have never navigated the college process, need extra support to close the information, opportunity, and attainment gap.

And as complex, demanding, and stressful as the process is, pursuing a postsecondary pathway is a non-negotiable in this global 21st century economy. In this decade, writings, research, and initiatives abound in the United States, alerting us all of the critical demands of the future work force, and the need for current students to pursue at the least, some postsecondary education, so that they too have the opportunities to live the *American Dream* as adults.

How to create college and postsecondary pathways for children is a question for all communities and citizenry to heed. Complex questions present multifaceted responses and resources.

Dr. Amanda Sterk offers just such resource in this guidebook, *College UnMazed: YOUR GUIDE THROUGH THE FLORIDA COLLEGE & UNIVERSITY SYSTEM.*

Presented in this helpful publication, you will find an in-depth resource for school counselors, college counselors, teachers, administrators, parents and families, community leaders, and students to use. This guidebook is just that, a detailed, superbly organized, nuts and bolts 'how to', for navigating pathways to postsecondary education. Helpful for the reader are both general and specific steps, many resources, and information relevant to Floridians. Follow the guidebook steps beginning in 9th grade to post-senior summer, and students will find themselves on the front steps of a college campus. Insights for those small tasks that can make a big difference are provided. Exploration of schools, types of schools, definitions of terms, the application process, financial aid and scholarships, all are detailed in an easy to read guide and reference for what to do, and when to do it.

I hope readers will use this book, as this is a helpful tool to close the information gap and support families and students from becoming entangled in the intricacies of navigating the pathway to further education. Ultimately, our Florida students, their future families, and all our communities across the state will benefit. Thank you, Amanda Sterk, for providing such a helpful resource for students and families.

And now – students and your families - turn the page, and begin creating your pathway to college. You will have **COLLEGE UNMAZED** by the final page.

Best wishes and much success to each user of this Guidebook on your life journey.

Rebecca A. Schumacher

Rebecca A. Schumacher, Ed.D.

Florida School Counselor Association

Executive Director

TABLE OF CONTENTS

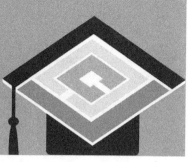

Look for these icons:

 Your Key to Success

 Helpful Links

 Additional terminology in Chapter 5

CHAPTER 1
ACADEMIC PLANNING FOR HIGH SCHOOL

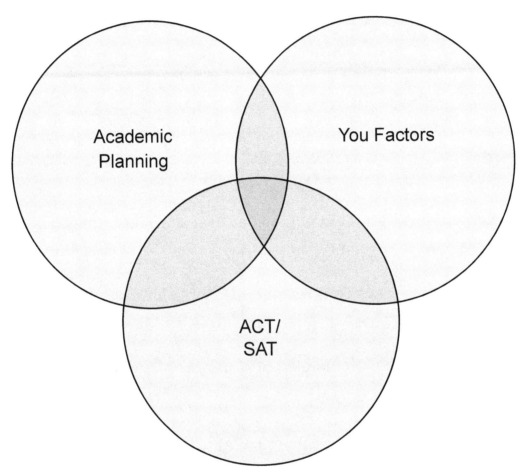

Academic Planning

You Factors

ACT/ SAT

HIGH SCHOOL ACADEMIC PLANNING

This *College UnMazed Guidebook* was specifically designed to help parents and students through the high school to college process with as little stress and as much ease as possible.

As parents and students we ask, are we on the right track academically to be accepted into colleges or to earn the scholarships we need to make college affordable?

As you begin this process, here are some things to ask and consider to ensure you make the right high school academic plan.

I. Begin Planning Early

In most school districts, there are a variety of different schools out there for everyone, with many different academic and extra-curricular activities. Even in small schools with little choice, there are many things that parents are just not aware of, so they do not ask the right questions. Knowing the names of programs and what is available either at the high school, off-campus, or online can be instrumental in the academic planning process.

Planning is the key to ensuring your student has the best possible situation they are able to have. You do not want to say at the end of it, "I didn't know they had that opportunity."

II. Questions to Complete by Asking Yourself, School, & Local Community

1. What type of student am I? Am I more interested in a career/technical path or a college to career path?

2. What are my high school graduation requirements?

3. What programs does the school have access to that helps me reach my career goals?

4. How can I combine my coursework so it works for me; such as Advanced Placement with Dual Enrollment?

5. When can I start these programs and what is required to get in?

6. What do *most* students who complete this program receive at the end?

7. If college credit can be earned, how does that happen?

8. How can I maximize in-school time and outside of school time like online, summer, and evening programs?

9. What types of programs are the colleges I want to attend looking for on a transcript?

III. Follow the Student's Passion & Motivation

If you do have choices in your schools (which most people do, it just takes a bit of work to find out what they are), do your research and compare what opportunities are available to you. If you are passionate about animals, a school with a vet tech program or an FFA (Future Farmers of America) program could make a huge impact on you. If you are dreaming of being an engineer or doctor, finding schools that can allow high levels of math and science courses to be taken is imperative for competitive college admission.

Unique College & Career Programs in Florida High Schools

COLLEGE CREDITS	CAREER & TECHNICAL
Dual Enrollment (on or off campus)	CAPE Digital Tool Certifications
Early Admission	CAPE Industry Certifications
Advanced Placement	CAPE Acceleration Industry Certifications
International Baccalaureate	
Cambridge AICE	
CLEP	

Most Popular Industry Certifications[1]

- Adobe Certified Associate (ACA) - Photoshop
- Microsoft Office Specialist (MOS) - Bundle Certification
- Adobe Certified Associate (ACA) - Dreamweaver
- Certified Food Protection Manager (ServSafe)
- Certified Internet Web (CIW) - Internet Business Associate
- Adobe Certified Associate (ACA) - Premiere Pro
- Certified Medical Administrative Assistant (CMAA)
- Adobe Certified Associate (ACA) - Flash
- Autodesk Certified User - Autodesk Inventor
- Certified Nursing Assistant (CNA)

---

[1] According to Florida Department of Education (FLDOE, 2016).

IMPORTANCE OF GRADE POINT AVERAGE

The National Association for College Admission Counseling (NACAC) states, "Students' grades and the academic rigor of their course loads weigh more heavily in decisions to admit than standardized test scores, high school class rank, or demonstrated interest in attending."[2] Also, "For high school seniors applying to college, performance in core classes is especially significant, with 79.2 percent of institutions attributing "considerable importance" to grades in college-prep courses. In comparison, 55.7 percent of colleges placed the same level of significance on admission test scores for first-time freshmen applicants[3] (see page 64 for admissions graph).

Recalculated GPA

Now that we know that grades are the most important factor in college admission, there is one more thing to know to be able to maximize that GPA. What many students and parents do not realize is that not all grades are created equal. Colleges and universities look at your grade point average differently than your high school.

I want to demystify some of the myths (if you even knew there were any!) about a student's GPA and how colleges use them.

Words to Know for This Section

Unweighted	This simply means the student does not receive any extra points for more rigorous courses like honors, dual enrollment, Advanced Placement, and so forth. An A in PE would be the same as an A in AP Human Geography.
Weighted	This GPA takes into account a student's rigor of coursework. More points are awarded for more rigorous courses. The more rigor, the more points. Student class rankings are often determined off this.
Academic Core	These include all courses taken in English, Social Studies, Mathematics, Sciences, and Foreign Language.
Academic Electives	This is sort of a gray area in college admissions. These are courses that students elected to take but are more academic. Examples would be Psychology, Human Geography, or Speech. Typically these courses are included in the recalculation.
Electives	Electives are the courses that do not fall in the core courses. These include classes like physical education, computer, business, arts, and study hall.

---

[2] Ivory, 2016, para. 4.
[3] Ivory, 2016, para. 6.

What to Know

1. Not all high schools use the same system! Some high schools use weighted or unweighted, while some do not even use the traditional 4.0 scale. This is why many schools will recalculate all GPAs based on the scale they want.

2. Colleges look at and use courses differently in recalculating the GPA.

    a. Some colleges will look at ALL course work taken. This includes not only academic core but all electives. Your student may have got an A in AP English, but why did they fail PE? That shows poorly in maintaining your responsibilities. Typically what is on your transcript is what they use.

    b. Some colleges look only at the academic core as part of the recalculation.

    c. Some colleges look at academic core and academic electives.

3. Most colleges use the weighted GPA as the best indicator for college success. Why? Well, the more rigorous courses you took in high school and did well in are often a good indicator to how you will do in college. One director of admissions said this, "We put more weight on GPA than standardized tests (ACT/SAT) because we would rather have four years of grit than one day of good test taking."

4. Colleges also look at what opportunities were afforded to you. Typically your school counselor has sent in a school profile that details what advanced courses they give, average test scores, and school programming. This is important for those in small schools that might not have a lot of specialized classes; admissions often compare you to your fellow peers, not you to other schools. However, while you may attend one high school, a lot of time there are multiple opportunities to take more advanced courses online or through Dual Enrollment.

Recalculating GPAs

So how does it work … let's take a look at some hypothetical students and see how they would fair in college admissions. In these examples, I have used what the Florida State University System has stated they use for weighting (+1.0 for all Dual Enrollment, AP, IB, AICE & AVID credits, and +0.5 for honors).

Student #1

Class	Grade	Unweighted	Weighted	Recalculated	College Credits
AP English	B	3.0	4.0	4.0	3.0*
AP Physics	B	3.0	4.0	4.0	3.0*
Psychology	A	4.0	4.0	4.0	0
Weight Lifting	A	4.0	4.0	N/A	0
Pottery	A	4.0	4.0	N/A	0
Honors Prob. & Stats.	C	2.0	2.5	2.5	0
Average		3.3	3.75	3.625	6.0

Depends on final exam score and the attending college.

What you see here is this student has taken on some AP courses and it helps in the weighted GPA. While receiving a B in those classes, the extra 1.0 added to the recalculated GPA by the university makes it equal to a regular course at an A. What you can also see is taking out the electives of weight lifting and pottery, reduced the overall recalculated GPA, because those A's do not count.

Student #2

Class	Grade	Unweighted	Weighted	Recalculated	College Credits
English	B	3.0	3.0	3.0	0
Pre-Calculus	B	3.0	3.0	3.0	0
Psychology	A	4.0	4.0	4.0	0
Weight Lifting	A	4.0	4.0	N/A	0
Pottery	A	4.0	4.0	N/A	0
Economics	C	2.0	2.0	2.0	0
Average		3.3	3.3	3.0	0.0

While this student is similar and still taking all the requirements for high school graduation, by not taking on more rigorous courses and not as many core classes, their GPA actually went down once you take out the electives. They become a less competitive student than Student #1.

Student #3

Class	Grade	Unweighted	Weighted	Recalculated	College Credits	College GPA
Composition	B	3.0	4.0	4.0	3.0	3.0
Intro to Psych	B	3.0	4.0	4.0	3.0	3.0
Intro to Biology	A	4.0	5.0	5.0	4.0	4.0
Statistics	A	4.0	5.0	5.0	3.0	4.0
Intro to Philosophy	A	4.0	5.0	5.0	3.0	4.0
Average		3.6	4.6	4.6	16.0	3.6

This final student is doing a full-time early admission program at their local state college. You can see that while taking fewer classes, the focus on the core work, coupled with the higher GPA weight makes them a very strong candidate for college admissions.

Things to Note

1. Not all college credits transfer to certain schools, so be sure the check with admissions. Usually these are very selective universities and out-of-state schools.

2. GPA for college admission goes from 9th to 11th grade, but includes any high school credit course taken before 9th grade (example: 8th grade Algebra 1, Spanish). However, you do have to put in what courses the student will be taking their senior year. Admissions do look for a continuation or increase of rigor … it is definitely not a time to get "senioritis" or to slack off in the core area. Some schools may ask for your mid-term transcript to ensure you stay on track.

3. Unlike the Student #1 and Student #2, Student #3 is creating a college transcript, as well as their high school transcript. If the student does poorly in a dual-enrollment/college course, it will be on their official college transcript and can negatively impact their college admission decisions.

4. As a reminder, GPA is only ONE factor colleges look at when deciding if students would be successful at their college. Other factors include ACT/SAT scores, extra-curriculars, and personal story. But if you plan well by taking more core classes and more rigorous courses, you will be at an advantage going into the admission cycle.

ACADEMIC FOUR-YEAR PLAN

The core areas create your recalculated GPA, which is what many universities use to judge for college admissions. To be competitive, the more courses in these areas and at higher levels (honors and college-level), the higher the recalculated GPA.

	9th	10th	11th	12th
Math				
English				
Social Studies				
Science				
Foreign Language				
Academic Electives *Depends on the college				
Electives				
Unweighted GPA				
Weighted GPA				

Your calculation might not be exactly right, but it gives you a quick understanding where you are with admissions.

THE "YOU" FACTOR

Colleges look at two factors of students applying: ACADEMICS and "YOU."

The Academic Factor is what was just described—your courses taken while in high school. The more rigorous courses and better grades in those courses, the more likely you will be successful in college. Colleges use these statistics to compare students for admission and scholarships. College admissions state this is the number one thing they use to determine admission.

The "YOU" Factor is what makes each student stand out based on their own interests and passions. The YOU Factor is what many universities, who use selective admission (meaning they look at both ACADEMIC and YOU factors) to make their college decision.

Become a "T-Shaped" Student

Often parents and students hear the myth that students need to be well-rounded for college admissions! It is just that, a myth. In terms of admissions, it is better to be a "T-Shaped" student.

College admission is changing as colleges and universities are becoming more selective in the types of students they take in. As adults, we believed the secret recipe of students receiving admissions into student's preferred college includes a nice mix of community service, school clubs, athletics, and sprinkled in, a few advanced honors or college courses, like Advanced Placement or dual-enrollment. Unfortunately, the problem with a student being well-rounded is that they usually lack focus or a specialized skill set.

College admissions today are looking for applicants who showcase two strong attributes. First, they want to see a strong passion for specific coursework, school activities, community engagement, or extra-curricular work. They prefer students with three or four strong activities or areas of interests for a prolonged period of time to show a continued passion and deep understanding, rather than a lazy interest. Second, they also want to see a broad set of skills to be able to work across multiple disciplines with ease and confidence. "T" students know how to work in small teams, solve problems, and show initiative and persistence to keep going when issues arise.

Here are some of the best ways to create a "T-shaped" student:

1. **Growth before Grades.** Many times, as parents, we put added pressure on our students to obtain a certain grade point average to enter into college. While important, college admissions would rather find students who have faced adversity, struggled in a more rigorous class, and learned to overcome. Learning should come from having a growth mindset by taking risks and triumphing.

2. **Specialized Coursework.** High schools in the area offer a wide array of coursework to allow you to specialize in areas in which you are interested and excel. If you are interested in being in the medical field, your transcript should showcase courses such as biology, chemistry, anatomy, and physiology. Taking on advanced coursework in a specific field shows you are willing to stretch to meet your future career goals. Students could also look at online courses, often free, such as Coursera, edX, Lynda, Alison, and Udemy that provide coursework from experts from universities like MIT, Berkeley, and Harvard from a range of topics like coding, medical neuroscience, business, and psychology.

3. **Internships/Volunteer Work.** There are many opportunities for students to receive hands-on experiences throughout the many programs in the area. While there are multiple opportunities to travel abroad and take part in various summer programs, having students take part in their field of study shows admissions they are willing to work at pursuing their interests. A recent senior I worked with wanted to be a naval architect. While he was accepted into a very high-priced summer program, the cost was just too much. Instead, we made a few phone calls and a local specialty boat-making company offered him an internship to do what he loves—build boats. He loved his summer experience, and used it as his college essay and recommendation.

4. **Part-time Work.** While finding part-time work for a teenager often won't be in their field of choice, working in a collaborative, fast-paced work environment will show admissions those broad set of skills they are looking for such as responsibility, time management, and work ethic.

5. **Extracurricular Activities.** The local schools and community have large amounts of activities students can be involved in. Students become involved in activities such as sports, martial arts, music, art, theatre, debate, and technology. Find something you are dedicated to being actively involved for a long, extended period of time rather than a large variety of activities to which you are not committed.

MY RESUME

Your high school resume builds the foundation of your applications. There are three reasons to use a resume:

*   A resume can guide your high school experience to the desired major and career path in which you are interested. By adding information as you go, it will be easier to have a clear picture of what your interests are and fill in holes where your college application might be lacking.

*   By starting early, you do not forget all of the activities you have done while in high school.

*   You use a resume as part of the application process. Instead of writing out all your activities on every single application, your resume helps you organize your information, edit it, and put the best activities/information forward. This is a KEY part to the application process. Use the adults around you to help you edit it, so you are putting your best foot forward on every application.

- Keep resume to one to two pages for a high school student.

- Use resume paper (if doing a hard copy) or plain white paper with font 11 or 12–definitely no smaller than 10.

- Avoid clutter on the page–be succinct with most recent activities listed first, oldest last on the list.

- At the end, you can put the date completed or revised in lower right hand to show that the resume is current.

- Have 2 people proofread and give feedback for clarity and ease of reading.

Helpful Tips on Resume Development

Resumes are as unique as the people who write them, but certain conventions should be followed. Here is a checklist of what to include.

- **Objective**. What are you trying to achieve: for example, major, minor, career, or type of college.

- **Education Information**. This includes the name and address of the student's high school, GPA (if it's brag-worthy), and class rank (if you know it). College courses can also go in this section, if you have taken any.

- **Activities**. These can be in or out of school—for example, marching band, intramural basketball, or youth group at the student's church or temple. Especially important are any leadership roles you have taken in these groups.

- **Work Experience**. A part-time job with details, particularly if it's in your field of study.

- **Volunteer Experience**. Participation in a walk for cancer awareness or contribution to a science fair are all pertinent details.

- **Awards/Certificates**. Academic awards or awards in extracurricular competition—state wrestling champion or member of the top-ranking marching band in the region, for example.

- **Anything Else That Makes You Shine**. A resume is the one chance you will have to tell college recruiters everything they need to know. If something makes you unique and interesting, by all means include it. Fluency in a foreign language or proficiency in advanced computer programs may qualify here.

SAMPLE RESUME

OBJECTIVE

Earn acceptance and merit scholarships to top-tier universities in the state of Florida.

SUMMARY

- I am a hard and articulate worker.
- I am very quick to grasp new concepts, as shown through the breadth of clubs I've done.
- I am very empathetic and try to help others in any way possible.
- I am a natural leader and have held leadership positions in a variety of clubs.
- I am very civically oriented and always try to be an active participant in my community.

WORK EXPERIENCE

Babysitter, 2012-2017
Fort Myers, FL

I babysit for a variety of families and have experience with a large range of kids. I have babysat for children with both physical and intellectual disabilities, as well as for children aged 3-14.

Lawn Care Organizer, 2014-2017
Personal Business, Multiple Locations

I organized a small lawn mowing service in which I found clients and built my business.

Administrative Assistant, 2017
Fort Myers Pediatrics, Fort Myers, FL

As an administrative assistant at this pediatric office, I work alongside trained professionals to assure that the front office runs efficiently and effectively.

EDUCATION

XYZ High School, 2013-2017

Weighted GPA: 5.12 Unweighted GPA: 3.92 Ranked 2nd in class 3rd best high school in state, according to Florida Department of Education.

This is a STEM high school where I am currently dual-enrolled and will graduate with an associate's degree. In other words, starting junior year I have taken dual-enrollment college courses.

VOLUNTEER SERVICE

Hospital Volunteer, 2014 & 2015, 40 hours
Cape Coral Hospital, Cape Coral, FL

I interacted with and served patients by providing essential supplies like water and blankets. I contributed to the efficient functioning of the hospital by performing errands for the nurses, and I learned about how the hospital functions.

TOP Soccer, Cape Coral, FL, 40 hours, 2015-2017

In this program, special needs children are paired with a "buddy" who works with them and teaches them how to play soccer in a way specifically adapted to their abilities, physically and cognitively. The buddy I have worked with for the last few years is wheelchair-bound, and we have both been learning the best way for her to control the ball with her chair, and she has progressed immensely both in skill and motor ability.

Volunteer, 2013-2016, 20 hours
ABC Elementary, Fort Myers, FL

This volunteer opportunity allowed me to teach first graders the foundations for the rest of their academic careers, essentially allowing me to shape the minds of the future.

Senior Member, 2014-2017
National Honor Society, Fort Myers, FL

Through the National Honor Society, I have been able to reach out through the community through an assortment of opportunities.

Open House Volunteer/Tour Guide, 2015-2016, 20 hours
XYZ High School, Fort Myers

> I worked alongside the school staff to prepare an informative session for potential students three times a year. I speak in front of large audiences in the engineering lab, as well as guide tour groups throughout the building.

Classroom Coach, 2015-2017 35 hours
XYZ High School, 1234 Gate Parkway, Fort Myers, FL 33919

> I led the Algebra II and Statistics class alongside its teacher, and engage with students to help them more fully understand the material.

EXTRACURRICULAR ACTIVITIES

Key Club, 2013-2017, 85 hours

> Key Club is a volunteer/service based club that seeks to improve the community through different projects including, but not limited to canned food drives, helping build houses for the financially needy, and participating in STEM-related activities with elementary age students.

Worship Team, 2013-2017, 50 hours

> I collaborate with other high school students on their own instruments, working diligently to get everything in perfect harmony, to lead our youth group in song. I am a vocalist, piano player, and flute player.

Prom Committee, President, 2016, 20 hours

> As head of this club, I coordinated several different subcommittees, communicating constantly with each of them. We worked tirelessly to plan the event and decorate our venue in conjunction with our coordinator.

Math Team, 2013-2017

> I competed against other students in my area, through taking timed math tests and working in groups with my peers to solve problems as a team. In December of 2016, I was able to earn 14th in Statistics at the FGCU Math Competition.

Medical Explorers, 2013 & 2014

> I listened to many medical professionals discuss their careers and their day-to-day responsibilities. I was also privileged to observe a cholecystectomy, two hernia repairs, and two complete knee arthroplasties over the course of two summers through this program.

Karate, 2009-2017

Grades 6, 7, 8, 9, 10, 11: I joined this karate program when I finished elementary school and continued with it until my senior year. It taught me the values of handwork, discipline and commitment.

AWARDS/CERTIFICATES

Sportsmanship Award

I was the only member of the Girls' Varsity Soccer Team to achieve this award, for maintaining a good attitude and encouraging others in the face of defeat or adversity.

XYZ High School, Honor Roll

I made Honor Roll every semester for my hard work.

ATHLETIC ACHIEVEMENT

Girls' Varsity Tennis

I compete in matches across Southwest Florida and sometimes farther. This season, I was chosen to be captain, leading my teammates and friends on and off the field. We have been historically successful, winning the District Championship in the 2012-2013 season, and competing as semifinalists every season since. In 2013, I was selected to receive the Sportsmanship award for positivity optimism in the face of defeat.

PERSONAL ACHIEVEMENT

Bilingual in Spanish and English.

MY RESUME

[FIRST NAME] [LAST NAME]

OBJECTIVE/RESUME PROFILE

BRIEFLY SUMMARIZE HOW YOUR QUALIFICATIONS MATCH YOUR CAREER OBJECTIVE

_____
_____
_____

SUMMARY

_____
_____
_____
_____
_____

EDUCATION

_____
_____
_____
_____

RELEVANT HIGH SCHOOL STUDIES

LIST OF CLASSES AND/OR SKILLS, COLLEGE LEVEL COURSEWORK OR SPECIALITY CERTIFICATIONS

_____
_____
_____

EXTRA CURRICULAR ACTIVITIES

TITLE/ROLE, LOCATION, DATE RANGE, DUTIES

_____
_____
_____
_____
_____

TITLE/ROLE, LOCATION, DATE RANGE, DUTIES

_____
_____
_____
_____

HONORS, AWARDS, AND MEMBERSHIPS

HONOR/AWARD/ORGANIZATION, DESCRIPTION

_____
_____
_____
_____

VOLUNTEER EXPERIENCE

TITLE/ROLE, LOCATION/ HOURS

_____
_____
_____

SPECIAL ATTRIBUTES

_____
_____
_____
_____
_____
_____
_____
_____
_____

MEDIA & RESUME BUILDING

More College Admissions Officers Are Checking Your Instagram and Facebook

The likelihood that college admissions officers will check out your Instagram or Facebook in addition to your GPA and application essays is growing, according to a recent survey from Kaplan Test Prep. A surprising 40 percent of admissions officers say they visit applicants' social media pages to learn about them, four times the amount that did so ten years ago.

However, most admission representative respondents (89%) who checked student's social media pages said they did so rarely and on a case-by-case basis. Major reasons include wanting to learn more about an applicant's creative interests, verifying unusual or noteworthy awards, or investigating reports of inappropriate or illegal behavior, according to the survey.

The result isn't always bad news. While a third of admissions officers said they'd discovered something negative that hurt an applicant's chances of acceptance, the same percentage said they found details, such as leadership roles or community service, which reflected positively on an applicant.

What's more, as colleges have started using more "big data" to help make college admission decisions, and is not uncommon for admissions offices to track applicants' social media behavior to help predict how likely they are to enroll or succeed on campus. Some colleges can infer how interested applicants are by how many campus photos they upload or how many friends they have on the college's social sites for applicants. This is one way they find student's demonstrated interest, which is 17% of factors going into admission decision.

Today's tech-savvy teens should know their Facebook, Instagram, or Twitter persona reflects on their actual personality. But consider this survey as an important reminder:

> ## Don't put anything on social media that you wouldn't submit as part of your college application!

* NACA, 2016

FINDING YOUR "FIT" MAJOR

As you start this process, many students do not know which career or major they wish to pursue, making finding the perfect college more difficult. While others of you may be dead-set on where you are going and what you want to be, now is a fantastic time to reflect on your personality and needs for your future career. This page offers you a chance to explore many colleges and career paths.

When preparing for the college process, this is typically how students today make their college and career decision:

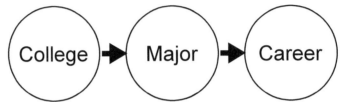

Why is this incorrect?

Statistics taken from CollegeBoard on college graduation rates found Florida universities are only graduating less than 66% of their students in four years! University of Miami was at the top at 66%, and University of Florida coming in fourth at 58%. This means a significant portion of students are extending into a fifth or sixth year of college. Not only is this expensive, as financial aid and scholarships stop, but time-consuming and frustrating. Current data from the Florida Board of Governor's Accountability Rate states 67% graduate within six years!!! The simple reason is that students enter college and change their major, affecting prerequisite courses and course sequencing.

What to do instead?

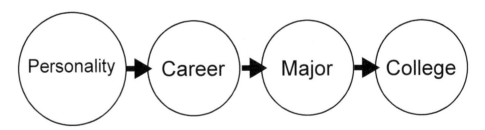

By starting with a student's personality first, it connects them to a career that they would be successful in based on what they would like to do. From there, they should connect those careers to what majors would lead to that career choice, and finally a college or university that has those majors.

---

[5] CollegeBoard, 2011.

[6] Miller. 2013.

This next activity walks you through that process. Take time to complete the assessments and answer honestly. If you do so, these assessments will give you a better understanding of who you are and what type of major/career is best suited for you.

PERSONALITY TO CAREER: DO WHAT YOU ARE

I. Florida Residents:
Explore your career and major through Florida Shines

 https://www.floridashines.org/find-a-career

Kuder Career Interests Assessment Results

1. Create a log-in to the site.

2. Fill out the survey instrument listed below (three of them).

3. Write down your Kuder Results (1-4)

4. Click on each result for specific information.

5. Write down four to six Occupation Names that each result gives you.

6. Explore interesting occupations through the website.

Top Career Pathways

Top Career Pathways	1.	2.	3.	4.
Occupation				
Occupation				
Occupation				
Occupation				
Occupation				
Occupation				

Kuder Skills Confidence Assessment.

Top Career Pathways	1.	2.	3.	4.
Occupation				
Occupation				
Occupation				
Occupation				
Occupation				
Occupation				

Super's Work Values Inventory

Your Top Values	Related Careers

II. College Board- Big Future

https://bigfuture.collegeboard.org/

Under Explore Careers, College Board provides some great resources on exploring careers and majors. Write down some of your findings from this website.

_____
_____
_____
_____

III. C'reer App

Download the C'Reer App for Android or iOS for free.

This three to four minute personality and vocational assessment identifies your interests and strengths. The app will then recommend the top career paths that match your profile. The app quickly scours all 5,000 colleges and universities in the United States to match you with the programs with the best track records for graduating professionals in those fields. Within minutes, you can be chatting directly with an Admissions Rep of a school that can get you on a career path of your dreams.

Personality Type: _____

Top Attributes (rank order)

1. _____

2. _____

3. _____

4. _____

5. _____

6. _____

Career Matches under Recommended:

Career Match	Schools

Reflect: Do you agree with the above results? Why or why not?

_____

_____

_____

_____

_____

_____

_____

_____

_____

_____

_____

_____

CAREER TO MAJOR

After using the assessments for personality traits to find the major of your choice, now we will begin looking at colleges that have your particular major. Meta-Majors Academic Pathways, created by the Florida College System represent the gateway courses that are aligned with a student's intended academic and career goals.[7]

 www.floridacollegesystem.com

Different Majors within a Career Path

Arts, Humanities, Communication & Design	Business	Education	Health Sciences	Industy, Manufacturing, Construction & Transportation	Public Safety	Science, Technology, Engineering & Math	Social Behavioral Sciences & Human Services
Digital Media	Accounting	Child Care Center Management	Dental Assisting/ Hygiene	Automotive/ Technology/ Service Management	Correction Officer	Computer Information Technology	Counseling
Graphic Design	Business Administration	Early Childhood Education	Diagnostic Medical Sonography	Aviation	Crime Scene	Computer Programming	Psychology
Liberal Arts	Entrepreneurship	Education	Emergency Medical Services	Building Construction	Criminial Justice	Engineering	Sociology
Mass Communication	Global Trade & Logistics	Exceptional Student Education	Health Information Technology	Engineering Technology	Fire Science	Environmental Science	
Multimedia	Hospitality & Tourism	Infant/ Toddler/ Preschool	Nuclear Medicine	Marine Engineering	Law Enforcement	Internet/ Networking	
Music Technology	Marketing	Middle Grades Education	Nursing	Professional Pilot		Life-Sciences	
Web Development	Paralegal Studies	Secondary Education	Pharmacy Tech			Pre-Med	
	Supervision & Management		Physical Therapy				
			Vision Care				

MAJOR TO COLLEGE

Use the following resources to find the college with your major.

CollegeBoard's Big Future website, under College Search:

 https://bigfuture.collegeboard.org/college-search

Cappex College Search:

 https://www.cappex.com/page/account/createStudent.jsp

Write down the top searches you found that meet your match.

Big Future	Cappex

TOP MAJORS AT FLORIDA SUS & PCUF

According to the Florida State University System (SUS) Matrix, which is a vital document that synthesizes the state university admission process, the following chart lists the top majors for each college. A similar chart on the next page lists the Private Colleges and Universities of Florida (PCUF) Matrix. As there are 300+ colleges in Florida, not all are represented in these charts.

SUS Top Majors Matrix[8]

	FAMU	FAU	FGCU	FIU	Florida PolyTechnic	FSU
Top 3 Majors for Undergrads	Pharmacy, Business Admin, Criminal Justice	Business Admin & Mgmt, Biological Sciences, Psychology	Management, Biology, Communication	Psychology, Biology, Business Admin & Management	Computer/ Mechanical/ Industrial Engineering	Biological Sciences, Business, Engineering

	New College of Florida	UCF	UF	UNF	USF	UWF
Top 3 Majors for Undergrads	Psychology, Anthropology, Biology	Psychology, Business, Engineering	Psychology, Biology, Mechanical Engineering	Psychology, Communication, Business Management	Biomedical Sciences, Psychology, Mechanical Engineering	Pre-professional Biology, Nursing, Business

---

[8] Florida SUS, 2016

PCUF Top Majors Matrix[9]

	ADVENTIST UNIV OF HEALTH SCI	BARRY UNIV	BEACON COLLEGE	ECKERD	EMBRY-RIDDLE AERO UNIV	FLAGLER COLLEGE
Top 3 Majors for Undergrads	Nursing, Biomedical Sciences, Occupational Therapy	Nursing, Biology, Management	CIS, Human Services, Business Mgmt	Marine Science, Env Studies, Int'l Business	Engineering, Aviation, Space Sciences	Business Admin, Communication, Psychology

	FLORIDA INSTITUTE OF TECHNOLOGY	FLORIDA SOUTHERN COLLEGE	JACKSONVILLE UNIV	JOHNSON & WALES	KEISER UNIV	LYNN UNIV
Top 3 Majors for Undergrads	Mechanical Eng, Aerospace Eng, Computer Science	Business Admin, Nursing, Biology	Business Admin, Nursing, Biology/Marine Science	Culinary/ Baking/ Pastry Arts, Sports Ent/ Mgmt, Criminal Justice	Business Mgmt, Int'l Business, Golf & Sports Mgmt.	Int'l Business, Sports Mgmt, Entrepreneurship

	NOVA SOUTH-EASTERN UNIV	PALM BEACH ATLANTIC UNIV	RINGLING COLLEGE OF ART & DESIGN	ROLLINS COLLEGE	SAINT LEO UNIV
Top 3 Majors for Undergrads	Biology- PreMed, Marine Biology, Business Admin	Biology, Pre-Nursing, Business Admin	Illustration, Computer Animation, Game Arts Design	Int'l Business, Psychology, Economics	Criminal Justice, Biology, Sport Business

	SOUTHEASTERN UNIV	STETSON UNIV	UNIV OF MIAMI	UNIV OF TAMPA	WARNER UNIV.
Top 3 Majors for Undergrads	Business, Communication, Ministry	Finance. Psychology, Integrated Health Sciences	Business/ Marketing, Biological/Life Sciences, Engineering	Marine Science/ Biology, Communication, Business Admin	Business Admin, Physical Educ, Natural Sciences

[9] PCUF, 2016.

COLLEGE STANDARDIZED TEST SCORES

I receive a lot of questions regarding the ACT and SAT tests—what they are, when best to take them, and what it means for college admissions. While a select group of schools are moving away from using standardized test scores for college admission, for most schools it is a big part of the college application. Not only is admissions connected to your score, but often times, scholarships are as well. A few extra points here and there can make a big difference.

In the state of Florida the following options for college entrance exams are available:

- ACT (all colleges and universities, selective dates, fee, paper-based)
- SAT (all colleges and universities, selective dates, fee, paper-based)
- PERT (only state colleges, any date available through institution, free, computer-based)

Basic FAQs

I. Should I take one of these tests?

If you are utilizing this Guidebook, then the answer is YES! Fortunately, you can take either test, and find which one is best for you.

Traditionally a student takes the PLAN or PSAT in 10th or 11th grade in high school to prepare. These are often given by the school and can be mandatory or employed as a sign-up process, but cannot be used for college admissions.

You must sign up for the ACT or SAT through the organization's website four to six weeks before each test date. Depending on your test-taking abilities and the type of school you want to attend, starting to take the test in 11th grade allows you the most opportunities to receive the score you need.

II. What's the difference between the ACT and the SAT tests?

While the ACT and SAT are both standardized tests that can help you get into college, they do differ a bit from each other. The ACT is focused on achievement, measuring the bigger picture of what you've learned in school, while the SAT measures aptitude, testing your reasoning skills and verbal abilities.

A common suggestion is to take both tests early on, see how those scores compare against what you need for the colleges you are considering, and then take the "better" score test again after more preparation. Unlike decades ago, universities have NO preference on which test you take—they care about your HIGHEST score.

III. How do I prepare for these tests?

A number of different ways are available to you for these tests. While your school may have test prep courses for you, going private can often be extremely costly. However, several good websites are out there that can give you diagnostic tests, flashcards, practice tests, and overall guidance.

Be careful of private tutors—make sure they are legitimate. Just because they charge a lot does not mean they are good or can get you results. On the other hand, you can learn certain strategies to be able to do better on the test. Knowing what the test makers are seeking for answers and shoring up some academic weaknesses could prove beneficial for you. Private tutors or computer programs can often help in this area.

One suggestion is to take the test first and see how you do as a baseline. On the second attempt, study on your own using some outside resources (for example, online, book, or at school). If your scores are still not what you need, then on the third attempt, consider some private, specialized tutoring to try and increase your score a few more points.

SAT RESOURCES

College Board

Four free practice tests are available through College Board.

Khan Academy

This online school has ACT and SAT prep. ACT primarily focuses you on math using algebra, trigonometry, and geometry principles with short quizzes. It also has study plans to get you thinking ahead for the big day.

Khan has partnered specifically with SAT to do their prep. This course is fantastic and free. It has math, reading, and writing examples and full tests are available. A recent study showed that using this resource significantly increased a student's test scores.

ACT RESOURCES

ACT

ACT just launched their ACT Online Prep. For $39.95 a year, you get an amazing diagnostic test that helps you hone in on your weaknesses.

Testive

This website offers highly individualized SAT and ACT preparation, as it chooses questions based on what you answered correctly or incorrectly to guarantee that you are always appropriately challenged.

OTHER RESOURCES

Princeton Review

Number one is SAT and ACT Prep books. These books are tried and true. They often connect students with free online versions of the full test. It also gives feedback on what your score would be, the correct answers, and a whole lot more. These books are worth the $10 to $15 investment to review the material.

Edupath (Mobile iOS App)

Edupath makes mobile apps with practice questions for the SAT and the ACT. The apps provide an extra dose of motivation by showing students what scores their top-choice schools require.

Other Options

- ACT Question of the day (Android)
- ACTStudent (iOS)
- The Official SAT Questions of the Day (iOS and Android)
- SAT Up (iOS)

IV. When should I take the test for the first time?

Typically, students will take the ACT or SAT during their 11th grade year. However, some students start earlier to begin practicing, and it can be used for certain high school programs, like dual-enrollment.

V. How many times can I take the test?

It's generally advised to take the test no more than three times, to avoid raising red flags with admission counselors. Prepare for the test as though you're only going to take it one time, and do your best. If you're not satisfied with your score, you can take it again.

For the PERT, some colleges restrict how many times you can take it and how far apart they need to be between each testing session. This is to ensure you follow a remediation process to increase your score. Contact your local state college for details.

VI. What if I have a 504 or IEP and receive accommodations?

If you have documented accommodations through your high school, you will need to go through your school counselor to receive them on test day for the ACT and SAT. They will need to fill out a form that includes uploading your 504 or IEP, outside documentation such as a psychological evaluation or doctor's letter, and added information. It is best to arrange a meeting three months before you wish to test to ensure everything is entered correctly.

The PERT is untimed and computer-based. Additional accommodations would be made through the testing center.

VII. What is the cost for the ACT and SAT tests?

These tests have several price ranges—one includes the full test with the writing portion or adding on subject tests. For Florida SUS and PCUF, the regular battery of ACT or SAT is needed, with no extra writing, essay, or subject tests. You may incur a late fee, if you miss the regular registration deadline.

ACT = $39.50	ACT with writing = $56.50	PERT = FREE
SAT = $43.00	SAT with essay = $54.40	SAT subject tests = $26

If you are on free and reduced lunch, there are waivers for both tests. You may use two for each test. You will need to see your high school counselor for this waiver. You are also entitled to waived application fees at some school universities, so be sure to ask!

VIII. Should I send my scores directly my desired college/university?

It will ask you in the beginning part of the two tests if you want to send your scores to a college/university of your choice. At this point, it is FREE! If you decide NOT to do so, and send it later, you will have to pay. ACT is $12 for each school sent, while SAT is $11.25.

IX. How do I sign-up?

You will need your six-digit school code. You select which date you want to take it and which high school.

 ACT- www.actstudent.org

 SAT- www.collegeboard.org

PERT - Contact your local state college testing center. Usually a link online will provide times in which you can schedule.

As a reminder, the ACT and SAT is just one aspect of your college admission. The following items also play a big part:

- Recalculated GPA
- Courses taken
- Extra-curriculars
- Overall college success

Use the College Planning Organizational Tool in the Chapter 5, *Resources,* to keep track of all usernames and passwords. This will save you time and stress later!

COLLEGE STANDARDIZED TEST SCORES

School code: # _____

1st Attempt, Date: _____

	Reading	Writing	Math	Science	Writing	Composite
ACT						
SAT						

2nd Attempt, Date: _____

	Reading	Writing	Math	Science	Writing	Composite
ACT						
SAT						

3rd Attempt, Date: _____

	Reading	Writing	Math	Science	Writing	Composite
ACT						
SAT						

Super Score: Highest from all categories

	Reading	Writing	Math	Science	Writing	Composite
ACT						
SAT						

ACADEMIC PLANNING CHECKLIST

A.   *Visit your school counselor early in your high school career and ask these 10 questions.*

1. What classes should I take, including core and electives?

2. Should I consider higher-level courses, such as Honors, AP, IB, Dual-Enrollment? If so, what do I need to do to get into those courses?

3. What other programs are available to me, either to receive college credit or work towards my career goals?

4. What standardized tests should I take and when are they? (If you have a 504 or IEP or receive Free and Reduced Lunch, ask the process for receiving accommodations and waivers for these tests)

5. What can I do to plan for college?

6. Are there any college fairs or financial aid nights being given at our school?

7. How can I start building my college resume at this school?

8. I'm not ready to commit to anything, but could you tell me about what kind of jobs and careers are out there?

9. Do you know about any good scholarships or financial aid?

10. Where do students from this high school often go for post-secondary education?

B   *Fill out Chapter 1 by working on your Academic Plan and College Resume.*

C. *Sign-up for the ACT, SAT, and/ or PERT (state colleges).*

CHAPTER 2
DEVELOPING A COLLEGE LIST

Chapter 2 is designed to walk you through starting to narrow down your list of colleges that best meet your needs. Documents include information on factors affecting:

- College Choices
- Finding Your Fit
- Reach, Just Right, or Safety Schools

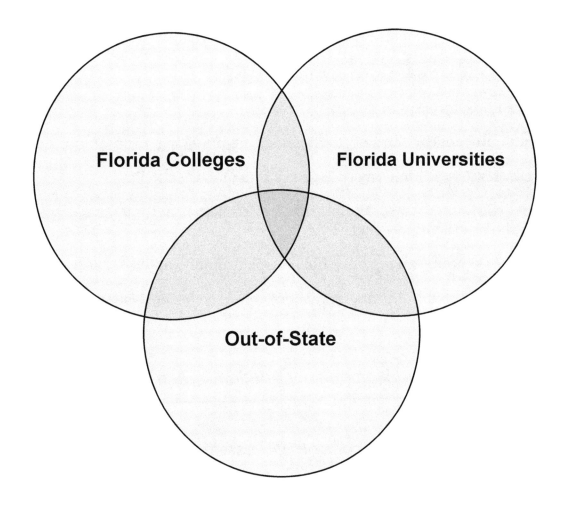

TYPES OF COLLEGES & UNIVERSITIES IN FLORIDA

Public State Colleges

Two- to Four-Year Degree & Certificate Options

Name	Location (Main)	Name	Location (Main)
Broward College	Fort Lauderdale	North Florida Community College	Madison
College of Central Florida	Ocala	Northwest Florida State College	Niceville
Chipola College	Marianna	Palm Beach State College	Lake Worth
Daytona State College	Daytona Beach	Pasco-Hernando State College	New Port Richey
Eastern Florida State College	Melbourne	Pensacola State College	Pensacola
Florida Gateway College	Lake City	Polk State College	Winter Haven
Florida Keys Community College	Key West	St. Johns River State College	Palatka
Florida State College at Jacksonville	Jacksonville	St. Petersburg College	St. Petersburg
Florida SouthWestern State College	Fort Myers	Santa Fe College	Gainesville
Gulf Coast State College	Panama City	Seminole State College of Florida	Sanford
Hillsborough Community College	Tampa	South Florida State College	Avon Park
Indian River State College	Fort Pierce	State College of Florida, Manatee-Sarasota	Bradenton
Lake-Sumter State College	Leesburg	Tallahassee Community College	Tallahassee
Miami Dade College	Miami	Valencia College	Orlando

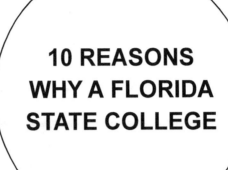

**10 REASONS
WHY A FLORIDA
STATE COLLEGE**

813,838 students currently enrolled

65% of high school students attend Florida colleges

28 colleges, 68 campuses, & 178 sites serve student needs

47% cheaper, on average, than Florida Universities

67% of students receive some type of financial aid

$31,375 average salary of Associate of Arts degree

54% of students entering Florida University System came from state college system

58% are minority students, making for diverse learning environment

88% of parents desire child to have post-secondary education

90% of state college students continue further post-secondary education or join workforce[10]

---

[10] FLDOE, 2016 & FloridaCollegeSystem.org.

PUBLIC UNIVERSITIES
Four-Year Degree and Graduate Options

Name	Location (Main)
Florida Agricultural & Mechanical University (FAMU)	Tallahassee
Florida Atlantic University (FAU)	Boca Rotan
Florida Gulf Coast University (FGCU)	Fort Myers
Florida International University (FIU)	Miami
Florida Polytechnic University (FLPoly)	Lakeland
Florida State University (FSU)	Tallahassee
New College of Florida (New College)	Sarasota
University of Central Florida (UCF)	Orlando
University of Florida (UF)	Gainesville
University of North Florida (UNF)	Jacksonville
University of South Florida (USF)	Tampa
University of West Florida (UWF)	Pensacola

PRIVATE UNIVERSITIES

Four-Year Degree & Graduate Options

Institution	Location	Institution	Location
Adventists University of Health Sciences*	Orlando	Johnson & Wale University*	North Miami
Barry University*	Miami	Lynn University*	Boca Rotan
Beacon College*	Leesburg	Miami Int'l University of Art & Design	Miami
Bethune-Cookman University	Daytona Beach	Nova Southeastern University*	Fort Lauderdale
Eckerd College*	St. Petersburg	Palm Beach Atlantic College*	West Palm Beach
Edward Waters College	Jacksonville	Rasmussen College	Multiple Locations
Embry Riddle Aeronautical University*	Daytona Beach	Ringling School of Art and Design*	Sarasota
Flagler College*	St. Augustine	Rollins College*	Winter Park
Florida Institute of Technology*	Melbourne	Saint Leo University*	Saint Leo
Florida Memorial University	Miami Gardens	Southeastern College*	Lakeland
Florida National University	Hialeah	Stetson University*	Deland
Florida Southern College*	Lakeland	University of Miami*	Miami
Full Sail University	Winter Park	University of Tampa*	Tampa
Hodges University	Fort Myers	Warner University*	Lake Wales
Jacksonville University*	Jacksonville	Webber College	Babson Park
Keiser College*	West Palm Beach		

*PCUF affiliated

OUT-OF-STATE COLLEGES & UNIVERSITIES

Though you may face financial challenges, as some colleges charge out-of-state students higher tuition fees than their in-state counterparts, attending a college far from home can be a very rewarding experience. You will get to explore new places, meet with people you wouldn't normally meet, and push the limits of your comfort zone.

But whether you have your heart set on a particular school or simply want to move elsewhere, the process of finding the right college, and getting accepted, can be more complicated for nonresidents than for others.

To help you make smarter choices when applying to colleges out-of-state, Admissions experts offer these tips.

1. Search for out-of-state scholarships and discounts.

While it's not the norm, some schools actually charge out-of-staters lower tuition than they do residents. New York, Minnesota, and South Dakota are among the states that, on average, offer cheaper tuition for nonresidents. See if your prospective colleges fall under this umbrella or consider applying to schools that do.

As an extra incentive to draw out-of-state students, many places provide scholarships for students outside their home state, sometimes matching in-state scholarships. Enrolling students from other areas of the country, as well as international students, often adds ethnic and cultural diversity to campus, so the Admissions Office works hard to draw you to their campus. Contact them to discover what kinds of scholarships you may be eligible for.

2. Consider private or liberal arts schools.

One option to consider is attending private colleges or universities that often have the same rates, whether you are in-state or out-of-state. As well, there are over 66 colleges and universities that are dedicated to providing 100% need-based financial aid, if a student qualifies. These are predominately liberal arts schools, but there are several national and regional universities as well.[11]

[11] Powell, 2016

3. Attend college fairs and regional open houses.

Attending college fairs at your high school or in your community are great ways to familiarize yourself with schools that you may not have of heard or have considered applying to. For instance, the National Association of College Admission Counseling offers free regional college fairs, at which students can interact with college admissions faculty. In Florida, these are in larger cities like Orlando, Tampa, and Fort Lauderdale with over 218+ colleges from all over the country and the world in attendance.

 www.gotomyncf.com

FACTORS AFFECTING YOUR COLLEGE CHOICES

To begin knowing what type of school is best for you, answer these questions:

1. Besides getting an education and preparing for a career, why are you going to college?

2. What type of college environment will challenge you to grow the most, academically and personally?

3. What are your top four to six criteria in selecting a college (i.e., cost, environment, activities, ranking, scholarships, financial aid, size, majors/ programs, location)?

4. In college, what extracurricular activities do you want to continue or begin?

5. What professions interest you the most?

6. List college majors that interest you *(see Chapter 1).*

7. What pressures, if any, are you feeling from yourself or others about going to college?

FINDING YOUR "JUST RIGHT" COLLEGE

This chart begins the conversation between parents and students on which type of college might be a good fit for each student.

Number the importance of each area on a 1-10 scale (1 = not relevant to 10 = deal breaker). Then write down your thoughts on each section, and why you wrote what you did.

Copy this page and have each person do their own. Then bring together final answers for comparisons. Be sure to ask questions of each other for clarification and write down final thoughts.

	Parent #1	Parent #2	Student	Combined
Location • Distance from home: —Far, near, in-state, out-of-state • Surrounding areas: —City, rural, suburban				
Size • Student enrollment • Physical size of campus				
Environment • Type of school (2 yr or 4 yr) • Co-ed, male, female • School setting (urban, rural) • Religious affiliation • Location and size of nearest city				
Academics • Your major offered • Student-faculty ratio • Research/internships • Typical class size				
College Expenses • Tuition, room and board • Estimated total budget • Application fee, deposits				

	Parent #1	Parent #2	Student	Combined
Housing • Residence hall requirement • Food plan				
Facilities • Academic • Recreational • Other				
Activities • Clubs, organizations • Greek life • Athletics, intramurals • Study abroad				

What are some areas you agree on?

_____

_____

_____

_____

_____

What are some areas you disagree on?

_____

_____

_____

_____

_____

REACH, JUST RIGHT, SAFETY

You can visit and apply to dozens of schools, but that's a poor strategy, as it is time-consuming and costly. Categorize schools into three categories:

- **Reach** - Your academic credentials fall below college's range for the average freshmen. Long-shots, but possible.

- **Just Right** - Your academic credentials fall well within (or even exceed) college's range. No guarantees, but it's not a stretch, or unreasonable to be accepted.

- **Safety** - Your academic credentials fall above college's range. You are reasonably certain that you will be admitted.

The rule of thumb is to pick six to eight colleges to apply to, with two or three in each category. Often schools that are just right or a safety provide substantial scholarships, making them a good choice for many students. Having all three types of schools on your list gives students and parents a wider net of information to make the final decision. Keep an open mind through this process!

KNOW THEIR ADMISSIONS!

1. Selective Admissions

Example: University of Florida - They want students who achieve in and out of the classroom, take advantage of student life, demographics, "holistic" (50% grades and test scores, 50% essay and resume)

2. Competitive Admissions

Example: University of South Florida - Based on GPA and test scores, scholarships that meet those levels, sliding scale or 50% GPA and 50% test scores.

3. Open Admissions

Example: Florida SouthWestern State College - Unselective and non-competitive admissions process, where the only criterion for entrance is a Florida high school diploma. Test scores (ACT, SAT or PERT) can be used for course placement.

5

FLORIDA UNIVERSITIES: FINDING MY FIT

With this exercise, I want you to see how you compare with competitive admissions, which means that focus is on grades and test scores, as they are at the University of South Florida. Things you should note:

They recalculate students' GPAs based on core and academic electives, so the GPA you see on the chart does not include any electives, but provides extra weight for all honors and college-level coursework. Use your recalculated GPA from your Academic Four-Year Plan to help with this.

They use other Academic Success Predictors, such as:

- One or more math courses at the pre-calculus, calculus, or higher math level
- Three or more natural science courses (two with lab)
- Additional foreign language course(s) beyond two sequential years of the same language
- College level dual enrollment coursework and grade point average (two or more courses)
- Postsecondary GPA of 3.0 or higher in all dual enrollment coursework attempted
- Strength of curriculum
- Grade trend
- Personal statements and letters of recommendation
- Background, special talent

There are MANY more colleges and universities in Florida—over 300!!
The schools presented here are part of formal groups, such as the
State University System or the Private Colleges & Universities of Florida.
Other schools follow similar application processes.
Contact each website on specific school information.

USF Initial Guidelines for Freshman Admission 2016-2017

Recalculated GPA

Composite Scores

SAT	>=1490	1420-1480	1350-1410	1280-1340	1240-1270	1200-1230	1160-1190	1130-1150	1100-1120
ACT	>=33	31-32	29-30	27-28	26	25	24	23	22
>=4.30									
4.20-4.29									
4.10-4.19									
4.00-4.09									
3.90-3.99									
3.80-3.89									
3.70-3.79									
3.60-3.69									
3.50-3.59									
3.40-3.49									
3.30-3.39									
3.20-3.29									
3.10-3.19									
3.00-3.09									

Circle where your scores fall!

Student will be admitted by USF for the fall, if USF fall minimum test scores match mine.

Student may be considered for summer programs if eligible, including the Summer Academy and Cultural Engagement Program (ACE) and the Student Support Services Program (SSS). Student may also be considered for alternative term admissions (summer or spring) or decision may be deferred for first semester grades and updated test scores.

Ask yourself:

Where do I fall on the chart?

_____

_____

What other academic success factors might I have for me to gain admissions?

_____

_____

What do I have that could be used for college admissions?

_____ One or more math courses at the pre-calculus, calculus, or higher math level

_____ Three or more natural science courses (two with lab)

_____ Additional foreign language course(s) beyond two sequential years of the same language

_____ College level dual enrollment coursework and grade point average (two or more courses)

_____ Post-secondary GPA of 3.0 or higher in all dual enrollment coursework attempted

_____ Strength of curriculum

_____ Grade trend

_____ Personal statements and letters of recommendation

_____ Other factors (socioeconomic factors, first-generation-to-college, family educational background, special talent)

Is this a REACH, JUST RIGHT, or SAFETY school?
(Circle one.)

FLORIDA UNIVERSITIES: FINDING MY FIT SUS

Mark as REACH, JUST RIGHT, or SAFETY, according to your academics.

	FAMU	FAU	FGCU	FIU	Florida PolyTechnic	FSU
Application Type	Selective	Selective	Competitive	Competitive	Competitive	Selective
GPA	Recalculated, core & academic electives, weighted	Recalculated, core & academic electives, weighted	Core & electives, weighted	Core & electives, weighted	Core & electives, weighted	Recalculated, core & academic electives, weighted
GPA Averages	3.00-3.50	3.73-4.37	3.42-4.22	4.0	3.5	3.9-4.4
ACT/SAT	Either	Either	Either	Either	Either	Either
ACT Summer Admit / Fall Admit	17-21 / 17-24	18-23 / 20-24	20-24 / 20-25	21 / 23	26	24-28 / 26-31
SAT (new)	RW: 501-600 M: 501-600	RW: 550-640 M: 530-610	RW: 560-630 M: 510-590	RW: 590 M: 590	1170-1260	RW: 640-710 M: 600-690
*My Fit						

	New College of Florida	UCF	UF	UNF	USF	UWF
Application Type	Selective	Competitive	Selective	Competitive	Competitive	Competitive
GPA	Recalculated, core & academic electives, weighted	Recalculated, only SUS academic core, weighted	Recalculated, only SUS academic core, weighted	Recalculated, only SUS academic core, and 2 academic electives, weighted	Recalculated, core and academic electives, weighted	Core and electives, weighted
GPA Averages	3.71-4.31	3.7-4.3	4.2-4.5	3.6-4.4	3.83-4.39	3.6
ACT or SAT Requirement	Either	Either,	Either (November test latest)	Either	Either	Either
ACT Averages Summer / Fall	N/A / 26-31	23-26 / 25-29	27-32 / 27-32	20.5-23.75 / 24.5-29	23-26 / 26-30	22 / 24
SAT (new) Averages	RW: N/A M: N/A	RW: 620-700 M: 610-700	RW: 640-730 M: 620-730	RW: N/A M: N/A	RW: 550-620 M: 590-690	RW: 560 M: 547
*My Fit						

FLORIDA UNIVERSITIES: FINDING MY FIT PCUF

Florida private colleges and universities are a great opportunity for many students. The small atmosphere and individualized attention can provide a wealth of internships, study abroad, and research.

Often families are scared off by the "sticker price" of private schools, but soon realize that with large scholarship opportunities from the institution, the Florida Resident Access Grant, Bright Futures, Financial Aid, and other scholarships, they are often quite affordable.

REMINDER: Did you mark each school as a REACH, JUST RIGHT, or SAFETY, according to your academics?

	BARRY UNIV.	BEACON COLLEGE	ECKERD COLLEGE	EMBRY-RIDDLE AERO. UNIV.	FLAGLER COLLEGE	FIT
Application Type	Selective	Selective	Selective	Selective	Selective	Selective
GPA Averages	3.0 (unweighted)	3.5-3.0	3.2-3.6	3.8 (Eng.)	3.54	3.41-3.90
ACT Averages	20	N/A	23-27	24-29	24	24-30
SAT (new) Averages	944	N/A	1015-1225	1160-1210	1058	1090-1270
*My Fit						

	FLORIDA SOUTHERN COLLEGE	JACKSONVILLE UNIV.	JOHNSON & WALES UNIV	KEISER UNIV.	LYNN UNIV.	NOVA SOUTH-EASTERN
Application Type	Selective	Selective	Selective	Selective	Selective	Selective
GPA Averages	3.4-4.0	3.03-3.87	3.2	2.7-3.0	2.5-3.29	4.02
ACT Averages	23-28	20-25	NOT REQUIRED	18-22	19-22	22-28
SAT (new) Averages	944	N/A	NOT REQUIRED	950-1050	870-1069	1000-1390
*My Fit						

	PALM BEACH ATLANTIC UNIV.	RINGLING COLLEGE OF ART & DESIGN	ROLLINS COLLEGE	SAINT LEO UNIV.	SOUTH-EASTERN UNIV.	STETSON UNIV.
Application Type	Selective	Selective	Selective	Selective	Selective	Selective
GPA Averages	3.57	3.3	3.2-4.1	3.5	3.39	3.54-4.19
ACT Averages	23	N/A	25-30	23	21	23-28
SAT (new) Averages	1061	N/A	1150-1300	1033	1433 (old)	1068-1250
*My Fit						

	UNIV. OF MIAMI	UNIVERSITY OF TAMPA	WARNER UNIV.
Application Type	Selective	Selective	Selective
GPA Averages	3.6	3.4-4.0	3.1
ACT Averages	28-32	25	18
SAT (new) Averages	1200-1390	1120	865
*My Fit			

SCHOOLS I'M INTERESTED IN

	INSTITUTION	WHY?	REACH/JUST RIGHT/ SAFETY
1.			
2.			
3.			
4.			
5.			

CHAPTER 3
APPLYING TO COLLEGES & UNIVERSITIES

Chapter 3 is designed to walk you through the application process for both state schools, private institutions, and out-of-state schools.

Documents include:

- Checklists
- College visit information
- Types of applications
- Recommendation forms
- College essay practice

While there may be some differing requests for documentation and types of applications, this chapter will ensure the process is as smooth and stress-free as possible.

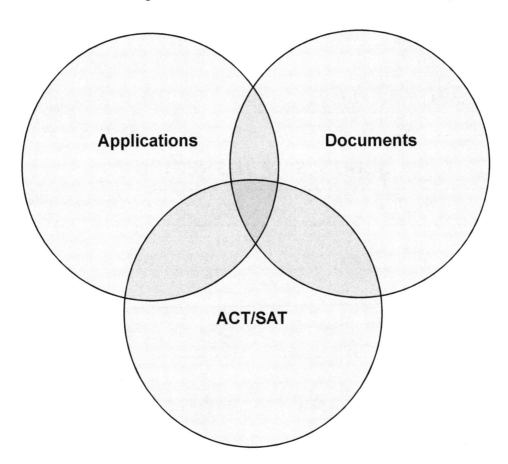

COLLEGE APPLICATION TIMELINE

9th-11th grade

_____ Begin researching universities and colleges you may be interested in.

_____ Check with your school counselor when college admission representatives visit the school, including during individual visits or college fairs. Receive their card and information.

_____ Begin corresponding with the college's admission representative.

_____ Schedule a formal or informal tour to visit the campus. Colleges also have open houses, or designated days parents and students may attend when additional activities are scheduled especially for visiting families.

12th grade

_____ Determine what type of application each school has; Institutional, Coalition, or Common Application (summer).

_____ Edit and finalize resume (summer).

_____ Edit and finalize essays (summer).

_____ Ask teachers and school counselor for recommendations (summer/early fall).

_____ Send in ACT or SAT scores to schools.

_____ Complete FAFSA (begins October 1st) and the FFAA (Chapter 4).

_____ Complete applications (preferably by the institution's Priority Deadline).

_____ Connect with college's Admission Representative to ensure all materials have been submitted.

_____ Talk with college's Financial Aid Office for any scholarships or financial aid opportunities.

_____ Apply for scholarships (Chapter 4).

_____ Receive acceptance letters! Celebrate!

_____ Receive denial letter—call and ask the college what is needed to be admitted (new test scores, summer or fall admit, mid-term transcript).

_____ Receive award letter (Chapter 4).

_____ Decide school by May 1st, submit deposits, and sign up for orientation.

_____ Request final high school transcript and, if applicable, college transcript, IB, AP, or AICE scores to be sent to college.

COLLEGE VISITS

Visiting different colleges is a vital process in finding what your student "fit" is. I have heard countless stories of a student's dream schools not measuring up once they got on campus. Are the buildings too old or too new, is the food bad, how about transportation, and do you see diversity? I have also heard the other side, where kids just stopping by found their school that just felt right. Whichever it may be, college visits are mandatory in this process!

1) *Explore the campus beyond the tour.*

While the campus may be big and beautiful, getting to know the town outside of the campus is a major part of the whole experience. Ask yourself questions such as, "Do I feel safe?"; "Where are such conveniences as the nearest Walmart, ATM, pharmacy, hospital, or art gallery?" This is very important to find that "fit" for you.

2) *Talk with current students.*

The tour guides are trained in what to show you and talk about. To get a true feeling of the campus, ask students in the campus common areas what they think of the school—both negative and positive. Think outside the box with your questions—I heard one person ask "What are the college's biggest warts and zits?" These questions will give you much more authentic answers than, "What is your favorite thing to do on campus?" And don't be embarrassed— they won't remember you! Ask away!

3) *Eat on and off campus.*

Food is important. Knowing your options can help you feel more at home. Do they have your favorite coffee and bagel place? Are there any options for special dietary considerations?

4) *Use a checklist and write down your thoughts.*

Use the checklist, "A Scorecard for Campus Trips," to keep track of all of your thoughts during your college visits. After you have seen several places, you may forget about some of the good and bad points of each school. Print this sheet and take it with you to keep track of the highs and lows at each school. It will make your decision come May 1st a much easier one.

5) *Stay overnight.*

Many colleges have some great opportunities to stay in the dorms, meet other students, and to "experience" college first-hand on their campus. Some colleges even pay for you to make the trip down by plane or car. These are fantastic opportunities to see the college up close and personal.

COLLEGE VISITS SCORECARD

Print one of these handouts for every campus visit you make. Be sure to write notes, to help you remember why you score the school as you did!

Choose a number system to keep track of how much you like the answers to the questions below (for instance, 1-5, 1 = doesn't work at all to 5 = perfect for me). Total the numbers at the bottom to compare.

Note that a lot of the college tours are done by students, so they may not know all the answers. Check out the college website, ask friends, and talk to an Admission Representative to complete your questionnaire.

A SCORECARD FOR CAMPUS TRIPS

School: _____

Location / Campus: _____

Academics

	How much time do students typically spend on homework?
	How much writing and reading are expected?
	Average class size of introductory classes?
	How widely used are teaching assistants on your campus?
	What is the average class size of upper-division courses?

Academic Perks

	Are there opportunities for undergraduate research?
	How many students participate in undergraduate research?
	Is there a culminating senior year experience?
	Do you have an honors college?
	Do you have a learning community or other freshman experience?

Academic Support

	What type of tutoring program do you have?
	How do you provide academic advice to students?
	Do you have a writing center and how do I access it?
	What kind of learning disability resources do you have?

Financial Aid

	What is the average financial aid package?
	What is the typical breakdown of loans versus grants?
	What percentage of financial need does the school typically meet?
	What is the average merit award?
	What is percentage of students receiving college grants?
	What is the average college debt that students leave with?
	What work-study opportunities are there?

Graduation Track Record

	What is the four-year graduation rate?
	What is the five-year graduation rate?
	What does it take to graduate in four years?
	What percentage of freshmen return for sophomore year (retention)?

Outside Opportunities

	How many students at the college get internships?
	What percentage of students study abroad?
	What type of career services do you have?

Student Life

	What kind of dorm choices are there?
	What percentage of students live on campus?
	How long are dorm accommodations guaranteed?
	How many students live on campus?
	Do most students go home on the weekend?
	What percentage of the study body belongs to a sorority or fraternity?
	What activities are offered to students?
	What clubs do you have on campus?

Other Considerations

	How far is it from home?
	Is the area around the campus safe?
	Do you need a bike or car to get to where you need to?
	How is the campus/public transportation?
	How are they going to use my FSW credits?
	Do I feel at home?

_____ **TOTAL SCORE**

AN INSIDE LOOK AT COLLEGE ADMISSIONS TODAY

If you are going through the college admission process, it is important to know what really matters in their college decisions. In a 2015 State of College Admission Report conducted by the National Association of College Admission Counseling (NACAC), colleges were asked to rate which admission factors were of considerable importance.[12] Refer to the following chart.

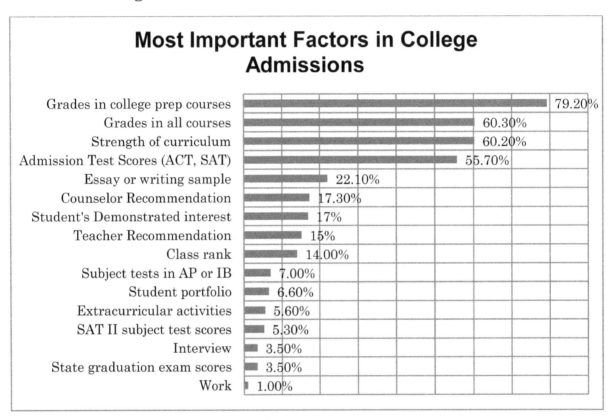

Most Important Factors in College Admissions

Factor	Percentage
Grades in college prep courses	79.20%
Grades in all courses	60.30%
Strength of curriculum	60.20%
Admission Test Scores (ACT, SAT)	55.70%
Essay or writing sample	22.10%
Counselor Recommendation	17.30%
Student's Demonstrated interest	17%
Teacher Recommendation	15%
Class rank	14.00%
Subject tests in AP or IB	7.00%
Student portfolio	6.60%
Extracurricular activities	5.60%
SAT II subject test scores	5.30%
Interview	3.50%
State graduation exam scores	3.50%
Work	1.00%

Other areas to note according to the report:

- Application volume is increasing about 6% every year
- 94% of students applied online
- Average selectivity rate: Freshmen 65.8%, Transfer Students 61%
- Email and institutional websites are primary means to recruit students, but also use campus visits, high school counselors, high school visits, direct mail, and college fairs
- 10% increase in students who apply for Early Decision & 7% for Early Action

Note: Only 30% of public high schools versus 73% in private schools have a designated college counselor.

[12] Clinedinst, Koranteng & Nicola, 2015.

MY COLLEGE LIST

Now you have done your research on both majors and colleges. Begin writing down the colleges in which you are interested and label what type of school it is for you (Reach, Just Right, or Safety).

Reach

1. Name:

Location: _____

Why it is a fit: _____

ACT/SAT/GPA Needed: _____

Application Deadlines: _____

2. Name:

Location: _____

Why it is a fit: _____

ACT/SAT/GPA Needed: _____

Application Deadlines: _____

3. Name:

Location: _____

Why it is a fit: _____

ACT/SAT/GPA Needed: _____

Application Deadlines: _____

Just Right

1. Name:

Location: _____

Why it is a fit: _____

ACT/SAT/GPA Needed: _____

Application Deadlines: _____

2. Name:

Location: _____

Why it is a fit: _____

ACT/SAT/GPA Needed: _____

Application Deadlines: _____

3. Name:

Location: _____

Why it is a fit: _____

ACT/SAT/GPA Needed: _____

Application Deadlines: _____

Safety

1. Name:

Location: _____

Why it is a fit: _____

ACT/SAT/GPA Needed: _____

Application Deadlines: _____

2. Name:

Location: _____

Why it is a fit: _____

ACT/SAT/GPA Needed: _____

Application Deadlines: _____

3. Name:

Location: _____

Why it is a fit: _____

ACT/SAT/GPA Needed: _____

Application Deadlines: _____

APPLYING TO FLORIDA STATE COLLEGES: CHEAT SHEET

The Florida State College System has made it easy to apply. Follow these simple instructions:

1. **Visit the college's website**

2. **Under Admissions, select the type of student you are:**

   - Freshman, First Time in College Students
   - Transfer Students
   - Readmit or Returning Students (this is for students who have attended before, like dual-enrollment)
   - International Students
   - Bachelor Degree Seeking Students
   - Dual Enrollment/Early Admission Students

3. **Apply online**

4. **Pay Application Fee ($30)**

5. **Submit high school and college transcript (if applicable)**

6. **Submit PERT, ACT or SAT test scores for placement into English, Mathematics, and Reading courses[13]**

7. **Provide additional documents**

   - Florida Residency Documents
   - On-Campus Student Housing

---

[13] All Florida State Colleges are test optional, if students have a Florida high school diploma.

APPLYING TO FLORIDA UNIVERSITIES: CHEAT SHEET[14]

Each Florida University has their own unique admission process.
Use this cheat sheet to determine what each college needs to apply.

	FAMU	FAU	FGCU	FIU	FLORIDA POLYTECHNIC	FSU
Application Type	Institutional	Institutional	Institutional	Institutional	Institutional	Institutional
Documents Needed	Two Recommendations & Personal Statement, Transcript, ACT or SAT	SSAR, Transcript, ACT or SAT	No essay, recommendation for scholarships & borderline applications, Transcript, ACT or SAT	Essays for scholarships & recommendations only, Transcript, ACT or SAT	SSAR & new video option, essay not required, Transcript, ACT or SAT	Two Recommendations & Personal Statement, Transcript, ACT or SAT
ACT/SAT	Either, not requiring ACT writing portion	Either, not requiring ACT writing portion	Either, not requiring ACT writing portion	Either, not requiring ACT writing portion	Either, not requiring ACT writing portion	Either, not requiring ACT writing portion
Application Deadline	March 1st	February 15th Priority Deadline	November 15th for Merit Scholarship, Rolling with Feb. 15th Priority	November 1st Priority Scholarships, March 15th deadline	November 1st, Rolling after January 1st upon space available	March 1st
Application Fee	$30	$30	$30	$30	$30	$30
Application Waivers	Waivers attach when submitting FAMU application	E-mail copy of official waiver or fax	Mail, fax, or upload to application	Mail, fax or uploaded to application	Mail, fax, or email	Waivers attach when submitting FAMU application

---

[14] SUS, 2016.

APPLYING TO FLORIDA UNIVERSITIES: CHEAT SHEET[15]

	NEW COLLEGE OF FLORIDA	UCF	UF	UNF	USF	UWF
Application Type	Common Application	Institutional or Common Application	Coalition Application	Institutional	Institutional	Institutional
Documents Needed	One Recommendation, Common App essay, Transcript, ACT or SAT	SSAR, short response (CA), ACT or SAT	SSAR, Coalition essay, ACT or SAT	Essay & recommendation not required, but encouraged, Transcript, ACT or SAT	SSAR, personal statement if borderline, ACT or SAT	Holistic review, Transcript, ACT or SAT
ACT/SAT	Either, not requiring ACT writing portion	Either, not requiring ACT writing portion	Either, not requiring ACT writing portion (November test latest)	Either, not requiring ACT writing portion	Either, not requiring ACT writing portion	Either, not requiring ACT writing portion
Application Deadline	November 1st Priority Deadline, April 15th guaranteed scholarship program	December 1st Priority Deadline for maximum FAFSA & scholarship review	November 1st. SSAR by December 1st, FAFSA by December 15th, Decision February 10th	Rolling	Modified rolling	December 1st scholarships and application, firm application June 1st
Application Fee	$30	$30	$30	$30	$30	$30
Application Waivers	Through Common App, high school counselor mails or sends	Mail or documents sent to uaoperations@ucf.edu	Respond in Coalition Application	Hard copy mailed to UNF admissions	Mail, fax, email, or uploaded to application	Email or mail letter from high school counselor expressing need

COMMON APPLICATION SCHOOLS

Several universities throughout Florida and the United States—nearly 700—use an application called *Common Application* or *Common App*. Some of these universities use this app or their own institutional app. Students may pick which to use, but no preference is given to admission from either application.

The goal is to *reduce* the amount of stress and time spent on applying to colleges, so if several of your schools utilize Common App, the ability to do **ONE application** for multiple schools is **HUGE!!**

Universities in Florida:

- Flagler College
- Florida International University
- Florida Southern College
- Lynn University
- New College of Florida
- Nova Southeastern University
- Jacksonville University
- Johnson & Wales University
- Ringling College of Art and Design
- Rollins College
- St. Thomas University
- Stetson University
- Saint Leo University
- University of Central Florida
- University of Miami
- University of Tampa

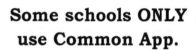

Some schools ONLY use Common App.

If you have a choice between Common App and an institutional application, if two or more the schools in which you are interested use it, select the Common App.

It is important to make a PLAN before you begin your applications, so you can minimize the work by maximizing all options.

If you are a student who receives free and reduced lunch, applications in Common App are waived, making it a great choice.

STUDENT SELF ACADEMIC REPORT (SSAR)

Question 1: What is the SSAR?

The SSAR is the student self-reported academic record that lists the courses and associated grades that have been attempted, or will be attempted, for high school and/or college credit. It replaces the high school and college transcripts used by the Office of Admissions during the initial review process. All freshman applicants, with a few exceptions, will enter their courses and grades in the SSAR. The SSAR should be submitted and linked with your application by December 1.

Question 2: Who takes the SSAR?

Currently, only the University of Florida, Florida State University, Florida Polytechnic University, and Florida Atlantic University are utilizing the SSAR. Once you complete your SSAR, please confirm with each institution on how to provide them with access to your data. For each school, be sure to both submit your SSAR through the SSAR system and link your SSAR data with your application.

Question 3: What do I enter into the SSAR?

Students will enter ALL coursework that was attempted for high school and/or college credit. For this, it is best to ask your school counselor for a copy of your transcript and academic history. The SSAR then recalculates your GPA as explained in Chapter 1.

If you are entering dual-enrollment credit, be sure to carefully read what you need to do and ask your school counselor if you have questions. If done wrong, your recalculated GPA could be wrong.

Question 4: Will I still send my transcript to universities who use the SSAR?

You will only need to follow the process of sending your high school transcript if you are admitted to the university. Otherwise, you will just need to complete the SSAR.

For further questions, visit the University of Florida's SSAR Questions at:

 http://www.admissions.ufl.edu/apply/freshman/ssar-faq

RECOMMENDATION PROCESS

Many universities and scholarships you apply to will ask for two academic references (a teacher or professor, school counselor), and sometimes someone that can tell of your character (coach, pastor, boss, internship/volunteer adults)

For Teachers & Counselor:

- Ask them first—they have the right to say no if it's not a good fit. Do NOT just send random links without asking.
- Be sure to know if there is a specific school protocol.
- They are writing about your academic achievements and to you as a "student." If there is any information you think they should know to write a better recommendation, provide that for them. Remind them of a story, or something you believe makes you stand out—let them know this. It is up to them if they wish to use it.
- For a counselor—they are providing a "holistic" picture. Be sure to let them know any personal barriers you may have had to give more context to your college application.
- Give them your Request for Recommendation Form and resume.
- If using Common App, you may send them a direct link to their email. However, be sure to ask them for a copy of the recommendation, so you can use it for other schools besides Common App.

For Outside Recommenders:

- You may ask for others that know you well.
- They are writing about your extra-curricular achievements and character—about you as a "person." This is similar to a teacher recommendation, so let them know anything specific you think they might use. Give them your Request for Recommendation Form and resume.
- If using Common App, you may send them a direct link to that email. However, be sure to ask them for a copy of the recommendation, so you can use it for other schools besides Common App.

Follow up with anyone who submits a recommendation for you by sending them a nice thank you note and a small token of appreciation.

MY RECOMMENDATIONS

This recommendation is typically needed for Common Application schools and scholarships. Recommendations are to strengthen your application. Admissions puts significant weight on these recommendations.

1. Counselor

Name:_____

Why this person: _____

Did I ask: Yes ☐ No ☐   Did I fill out the Counselor Form: Yes ☐ No ☐

Follow-up completed & small thank-you note/gift sent: Yes ☐ No ☐

2. Teacher/Professor

Name:_____ Subject Area: _____

Why this person: _____

Did I ask: Yes ☐ No ☐   Recommendation Form: Yes ☐ No ☐

Follow-up completed & small thank-you note/gift sent: Yes ☐ No ☐

3. Teacher/Professor

Name:_____ Subject Area: _____

Why this person: _____

Did I ask: Yes ☐ No ☐   Recommendation Form: Yes ☐ No ☐

Follow-up completed & small thank-you note/gift sent: Yes ☐ No ☐

4. Extra-Curricular

Name:_____ Subject Area: _____

Why this person: _____

Did I ask: Yes ☐ No ☐   Recommendation Form: Yes ☐ No ☐

Follow-up completed & small thank-you note/gift sent: Yes ☐ No ☐

Teacher Recommendation Request Form

Student's Name: _____

Today's Date: _____

Email Address /Phone # (in case of questions) _____

Teacher's Name: _____

Course(s) with This Teacher: _____

Thank you so much for agreeing to write this letter of recommendation for me. I asked you, because I think you are a teacher who knows me well and who can accurately evaluate my potential for academic success in college. This information may be helpful to you as you write the recommendation.

1. I think my academic strengths are …

    a. _____

    b. _____

    c. _____

2. I think my personal strengths are …

    a. _____

    b. _____

    c. _____

3. I am considering the following college majors, because …

    a. _____

    b. _____

    c. _____

4. Some things I want the college admission and/or scholarship committee to know about me …

    a. _____

    b. _____

    c. _____

5. The specific things I hope you discuss in this letter …

    a. _____

    b. _____

    c. _____

6. What I remember most about your class …

    a. _____

    b. _____

    c. _____

7. Additional information that might be helpful …

_____

_____

Students: Attach a résumé to this form, so a better recommendation can be written. However, remember that the teacher recommendation will focus on you as a student in this teacher's classroom.

I Am Applying to the Following Schools:

Name of School	Location

Again, thank you. I know this is a big time commitment, and I appreciate your help.

Sincerely,

COUNSELOR RECOMMENDATION FORM

One of the major aspects of your application to colleges is the written counselor recommendation.

Often times, students do not realize school counselors must submit a recommendation letter. Some applications require it to even send in a transcript! The more your counselor knows about you, both personally and academically, the better their letter can attest to your strengths and personality.

The counselor recommendation is used by Admissions to see if what the student said in the application is true and to fill in any missing pieces to the student's academic history.

For all counselor recommendations, include your resume and this form completed.

This Counselor Recommendation Form also helps you to start thinking of what makes you unique as a student. It allows you to see these characteristics as well to better prepare for your essay writing.

Take time and answer the questions that you think would best represent you or help tell your story, the more heartfelt and honest the better! Feel free to copy and paste so you can type your responses, or include additional paper.

Counselor Recommendation

1. What are your academic interests? _____

    Which courses have you enjoyed the most? _____

    Why? _____

2. Has there been any exceptional classroom experience that stands out in your mind?

    _____

    _____

3. What major or particular area of concentration would you like to study in college? Why?

    _____

    _____

    If you are unsure, then tell me some of the areas that you are interested in exploring.

    _____

4. What are your future career plans and goals? _____

    How did you determine them? _____

5. What activities or organizations do you think you might want to explore in college?

    _____

    _____

6. Have any unusual situations affected your academic performance like family issues, illnesses, or moving?

    _____

7. Please share one or more specific experiences you have had over the past four years that have had an impact on your life in some way.

    _____

8. Has any summer experience, work, or summer study program been of significant importance to you? Please describe the one that was the most meaningful to you and tell me why.

_____

_____

9. What do you consider your greatest strengths or talents?

_____

_____

10 What areas could you improve in? How would you do this?

_____

_____

11. What makes you unique? Choose three or four adjectives that best describe you, and tell me why you chose these words?

_____

_____

12. Is there any particular issue that you feel passionate about? (It can be school related, community related or society in general.)

_____

_____

13. Please tell me about your family background. (Whatever information might help me know you a little better.)

_____

_____

14. Is there any one person who has made an impact on your life? Why?

_____

_____

_____

COLLEGE ESSAY PREPARATION

One of the major pieces of the application process is your personal essay. Admissions Representatives state this essay is almost one-fourth of their overall admission decision![18]

The college essay is designed to provide the Admission Committee something that is unique to you. This does not mean you would restate your resume, but provide one well-written example of what is important in your life. If a college asks for a college essay, it is a "selective" school and uses it as a large part of their admission process, so it is important that it is well-written, free from any grammatical errors, and centered on the topic you choose.[19]

Eight Tips on Writing College Essay

1. Get started by brainstorming
2. Let your first draft flow
3. Develop three essay parts
4. Be specific
5. Find a creative angle
6. Be honest
7. Get feedback
8. Proofread and make corrections

[18] Clinedinst, Karanteng & Nicola, 2015.

[19] Refer to Canvas College & Careet Readiness for more essay example details.

Common Application Essay for 2017-2018

1. Some students have a background, identity, interest, or talent that is so meaningful they believe their application would be incomplete without it. If this sounds like you, then please share your story.

2. The lessons we take from *obstacles we encounter* can be fundamental to later success. Recount a time when you faced a *challenge, setback, or failure.* How did it affect you, and what did you learn from the experience?

3. Reflect on a time when you *questioned* or challenged a belief or idea. What prompted your *thinking?* What was the *outcome?*

4. Describe a problem you've solved or a problem you'd like to solve. It can be an intellectual challenge, a research query, an ethical dilemma—anything that is of personal importance, no matter the scale. Explain its significance to you and what steps you took or could have taken to identify a solution.

5. Discuss an accomplishment, event, or realization that sparked a period of personal growth and a new understanding of yourself or others.

6. Describe a topic, idea, or concept you find so engaging that it makes you lose all track of time. Why does it captivate you? What or who do you turn to when you want to learn more?

7. Share an essay on any topic of your choice. It can be one you've already written, one that responds to a different prompt, or one of your own design.

University of Florida Essay for 2017-2018

1. Tell a story from your life, describing an experience that either demonstrates your character or helped to shape it.

2. Describe a time when you made a meaningful contribution to others in which the greater good was your focus. Discuss the challenges and rewards of making your contribution.

3. Has there been a time when you've had a long-cherished or accepted belief challenged? How did you respond? How did the challenge affect your beliefs?

4. What is the hardest part of being a teenager now? What's the best part? What advice would you give a younger sibling or friend (assuming they would listen to you)?

5. Submit an essay on a topic of your choice.

Florida State University Essay for 2017-2018

1. Describe an experience from your life that either demonstrates your character or helped shape it.

2. Describe a time when you made a meaningful contribution to others in which the greater good was your focus. Discuss the challenges and rewards of making your contribution.

3. Has there been a time when you've had a long-cherished or accepted belief challenged? How did you respond? How did the challenge affect your beliefs?

Use the following pages to enter these ideas or answer some of the previous questions.

Brainstorm

- Interests
- Unique Experiences
- Goals
- Family/Student Background

FALL SENIOR MEETING WITH SCHOOL COUNSELOR

School counselors are busy, but they hold a wealth of information that will significantly help you through the college application process. Schedule a meeting with your counselor and parent(s). Being prepared with the following items will help you organize your thoughts and ask specific questions about your needs.

1. Have your resume completed and bring to the meeting.

2. Fill out the Finding Your Fit College Chart.

3. Have 8-10 schools in mind—you should have visited most, if not *all* of these colleges. Fill out My Fit assignment page.

4. Discuss "Schools I'm Interested In" and any specific programs you find interesting. Does the counselor think you have labeled your Reach, Just Right, and Safety schools appropriately?

5. Research and know deadlines and types of application (Institutional, Coalition, or Common App).

6. Have ideas of who your references will be.

7. Attend as many college visits (both on the college campus and at the high school) and college fairs as possible.

8. Have your Counselor Recommendation Form filled out.

Questions to Ask

1. What are some specific things that need to be done to receive recommendations and send transcripts?

2. How are college visits at the high school posted so you can attend?

3. What are some local and state scholarships you should be looking into?

4. What are some upcoming parent/student nights on Financial Aid, scholarships, essay review, or any other support activities?

5. Where are students with your academics going for post-secondary education?

6. Do they have any schools that would seem to be a good match for you?

COLLEGE APPLICATION TRACKING CHART

College	1	2	3	4	5	6
College Visit						
Type Of Application						
Type Of Application						
Application Completed & Submitted Date						
Transcript Requested						
Test Scores Sent						
Recomm.Requested						
Financial Aid Forms Filed						
Result						
Scholarship $ Given						

CHAPTER 4
AFTER APPLYING:
SCHOLARSHIPS & FINANCIAL AID

Chapter 4 is designed to walk you through what should happen after you apply to universities. This includes understanding the varying types of scholarships, as well as finalizing any decisions you may have.

Documents include:

- Scholarship and financial aid resources
- Checklists
- Additional online resources
- Yearly calendar (track deadlines)

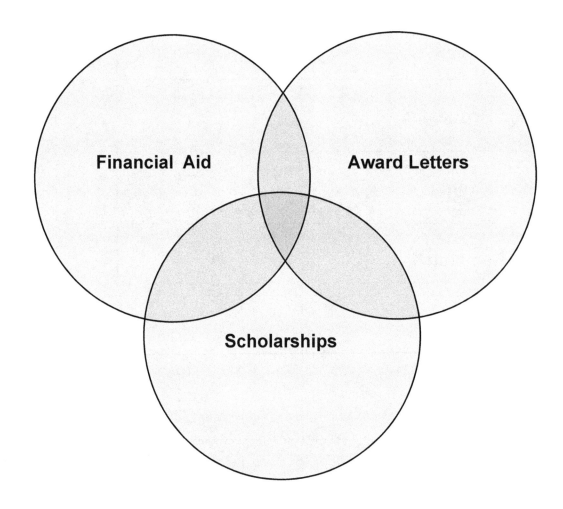

TALKING ABOUT MONEY

While it is tough to talk finances as a family, this is the time to sit down and find out where everyone is positioned when it comes to contributing to your post-secondary goals.

Questions to Ask

1. **What will you be in charge of repaying?**

_____

_____

2. **Do you need to borrow the money?   Yes ☐ No ☐   If so, how?**

_____

3. **What are your parents' expectations of you working during school?**

_____

_____

4. **Are there other alternatives to bring down your cost, such as living off-campus, not having a car, to meal plan or not meal plan? What are you each comfortable with forgoing?**

_____

_____

5. **What about incidental expenses, besides school supplies (BOOKS!), such as gas, pizza on the weekends, trips to Publix for Velveeta, and chips (I lived off that for my freshman year!), and "having fun" money?**

_____

_____

Also, finding money needs to be a priority—meaning, after you have submitted your applications, this should be considered a part-time job. With enough focus and dedication, more opportunities will come your way.

Once you know the net price you will need to pay, build a budget now before you select your school (specific cities are more expensive—how does this affect your budget?), and have this discussion. As a young adult, you have to stick to this plan, as it could mean racking up debt later on.

SCHOLARSHIP TYPES

There are five main types of scholarships out there that you should start looking for. Note that these scholarships are often "stackable," meaning if you receive more than one, they "stack" on the other scholarships, all going towards your college price.

Institutional: This money comes from the university to bring down the price of tuition, room, and board. Sometimes, because of scores and your demographics, you just receive them—other times you have to apply. Ask!!

Micro-Scholarships: **Raise.Me** has been a game changer for how universities give money. Instead of the old thought of apply, then decide, micro-scholarships are scholarships your student can earn in small increments throughout their high school career.

National: National scholarships are from large organizations like Coca-Cola, American Council of the Blind Scholarship, Siemens Competition, Don't Text and Drive Scholarship, and more! These usually have larger monetary value, but more people apply. Usually an essay, references, or something else needs to be done to be considered.

Federal: While not necessarily a scholarship, filling out the FAFSA (Free Application for Federal Student Aid,) can provide grants, loans, and access to scholarships that otherwise could not have been received.

 https://fafsa.ed.gov/

Local: Local scholarships come from the community where students live. While these scholarships are smaller in value than larger national scholarships, less people are applying for them making them very accessible to students.

State: Florida offers a state scholarship called Florida Bright Futures Scholarship to qualifying students approximately $1,800 to $6,000 worth of annual scholarships.

❺

INSTITUTIONAL SCHOLARSHIPS

Institutional scholarships are probably the most widely known scholarships today, but typically families only hear of the "full-ride." Many families do not know that universities give millions of dollars away every year to all types of students of varying award amounts. This money comes directly from the university or college to bring down the price of tuition, room, and board.

How do students earn these scholarships?

1. Students first need to apply to the university/college in question.

2. During the admission review process, they are looking if the student may be eligible for different scholarships depending on multiple factors, what I call "Academic Factors" and "You Factors", such as:

    - Grade point average (weighted, recalculated)
    - Standardized test scores (ACT or SAT)
    - Special talents and abilities, such as sports, dance, and music

    - Major of choice
    - Passions/interests
    - Ethnicity
    - First-generation students

3. If students meet one or more of the criteria, two things may occur:

    - Students are automatically awarded the scholarship
    - Students are asked to *apply* to the scholarship.

    Note: *This process could involve coming to campus, interviewing, writing an essay, submitting recommendations, or filling out an application. If asked to apply, it is extremely important to follow all requirements and deadlines. Follow through on all scholarship opportunities when given.*

4. If a student is to receive scholarships, the university may:

    - Inform the student personally
    - Notify students in their Awards Letter

5. When a student accepts the Award Letter, the scholarships will be directly applied to the tuition and/or room and board (depending on the scholarship type).

With any institution, families should scour the website to see what scholarships are available. It is also extremely important to build a relationship with the Admission Counselor and Financial Aid Office. Many times, just by asking provides important information. The key is—you must apply!

The next chart is a great example of how varying instituations give differing amounts of scholarships. While many families believe colleges are too expensive, you can see below that different colleges are able to tap into varying money streams for students, such as giving instutional scholarships and federal or state aid. The graph also shows that public versus private can vary greatly in how much is awarded and which type of scholarships are awarded.

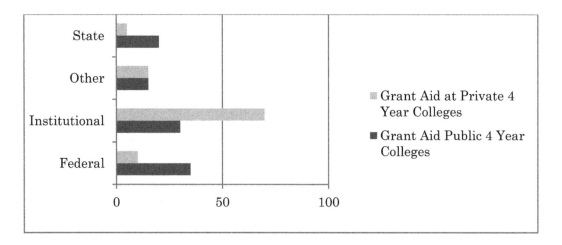

Use the College Board, Big Future College Search site under each individual college's Paying & Financial Aid by Numbers to see where each school stacks up in terms of financial aid and scholarships given.

See the following examples comparing how each institution distributes their financial aid and scholarships.

 https://bigfuture.collegeboard.org

University Scholarship & Financial Aid Comparisons

Florida SouthWestern State College Aid

- Scholarships/ Grants
- Loans/ Jobs

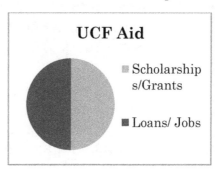

UCF Aid

- Scholarships/Grants
- Loans/ Jobs

$3,011 average need-based loan

$5,307 average-based scholarships or grant award

$3,190 average need-based aid

$6,005 average 1st year financial aid package

$3,616 average need-based loan

$5,824 average scholarship or grant award

$3,839 average non-need based aid

$8,516 average 1st year financial aid package

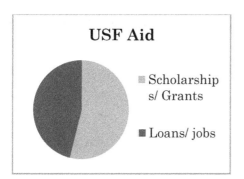

USF Aid

- Scholarships/ Grants
- Loans/ jobs

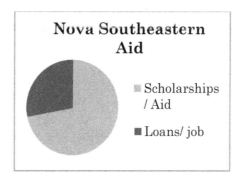

Nova Southeastern Aid

- Scholarships / Aid
- Loans/ job

$4,717 average need-based loan

$9,183 average need-based scholarship or grant award

$3,074 average non need-based aid

$2,803 average need-based loan

$18,553 average need-based scholarship or grant award

$12,779 average non need-based aid

$12,007 average 1st year financial aid package

$30,160 average 1st year financial aid package

When it comes to institutional scholarships there are several things to consider:

- Public vs. private
- Competition
- Options

Information taken from, Collegeboard.org

Public vs. Private

Public and private institututional scholarship money can vary greatly for the same student at different insitutions. What is often the "sticker price" is not always the "net price," meaning what is stated as the total cost comes out looking very different once you receive the award letter.

In the example on the previous page, you can see each post-secondary institution awards various amounts. By simply subtracting the *cost of attendance (COA)*, which includes an estimated cost of tuition, room and board, transportation, fees, and books, and then subtracting the average financial aid and scholarship packages yields the *net price,* or price families pay.

Institution	COA	Average Aid	Net Price
FSW	$16.611	$6,005	$10.606
UCF	$22,044	$8,516	$13,528
USF	$21,410	$12,007	$9,403
Nova Southeastern	$45,430	$30,160	$15,270

Information taken from, Collegeboard.org

Competition

I have seen parents able to reduce the price by just asking! No longer are students bystanders in this process. Universities and colleges are often ranked on students accepting the seat at the school and attending there. So it is often in a college's best interest to meet the financial needs of the student as much as possible.

I counsel students to apply to similar schools (particularly private schools do this), and if one gives a better scholarship than another, it is perfectly fine and acceptable to ask the other college if they can at least match the other offer. Often times they do! You don't know until you ask!

Options

Many students are choosing alternative options to reduce the cost of attending college. Options that many students consider are:

- Utilize college courses while still in high school, focusing on core classes
- Living at home or off-campus
- Attending a state college and then transferring to a larger four-year university
- Utilizing a college's online courses to maximize work time

MICRO-SCHOLARSHIPS

Micro-Scholarships are relatively unknown scholarship resources. In all essence, they are institutional scholarships, but packaged very differently. Instead of giving scholarships out *after* a student applies, micro-scholarship are earned *before* a student applies and accrues over time into very large sums of money. The website for micro-scholarships is:

 www.raise.me

Starting in ninth grade, students can enter a wide range of high school activities, such as:

- Grades (i.e., AP, IB, Dual-enrollment, honors, regular, core, or electives)
- Standardized test scores (ACT/SAT)
- Extra-curricular activities
- Volunteering
- Community Service
- Sports

Each institution then determines how much they want to give for each of the things listed below:

- Have an A in a dual-enrollment course? Here is $500
- Are you in the school play? Here is $1,000.
- Do you regularly do community service? Here is $500.

The amounts vary, but what happens is these small or micro activities, when added up, mean big scholarships. So the student above is already looking at $2,000 in institutional scholarships!!

What I love about this is that it motivates students very early on to be active and involved. They can immediately see how this pays off in free college money. Every student in the entire country should be on www.raise.me.

This is how it works:

1. Students enter in their information throughout their high school years.
2. Students will apply to the universities in their senior year.
3. Students must finalize the information by specific deadlines (around application time) through the website.
4. If accepted, the micro-scholarships will automatically be applied to the Award Letter.

It is that simple!

NATIONAL SCHOLARSHIPS

National scholarships are what families know and hear about through multiple websites. There are many websites out there that help you search for these large scholarships from organizations and businesses around the country and world. Searching for these types of scholarships can often be daunting and confusing. However, if received, these scholarships make a huge difference in the cost of college, as typically national scholarships can be used at any institution the student is going to, unlike institutional scholarships that are only good at the one particular school.

Two types of national scholarships are available:

- **Competitive** - Students are required to fill out an application which could include recommendation letters or an essay. Sometimes students need to attend an interview or event to participate. There is a committee that determines who should receive the scholarship.

- **Lottery** - Students simply fill out some information, and the search committee "pulls a name out of the hat" so to speak. Just chance—no skill.

Most of these websites "sell" your information, so you may begin getting bombarded with other offers. I suggest you create a separate college-bound email for this process that sounds professional and keeps things more organized. Both parents and students should have access to this account.

Websites:

- www.cappex.com
- www.scholarships.com
- www.fastweb.com
- www.Zinch.com
- www.ScholarshipPoints.com
- www.Cappex.com

Scholly App:

For just a few dollars up front you have unlimited access to scholarships, and they don't sell your information!

Tips:

- Do research early
- Be prepared (recommendations & essays)
- Know your deadlines

FEDERAL SCHOLARSHIPS

While *Federal Financial Aid* or FAFSA (Free Application for Federal Student Aid) is not a scholarship per se, it is a path to FREE money! In Florida alone, the federal and state government awarded *$2.3 billion* awarded to 651,550 students attending 286 colleges and universities in Florida.[20] Unfortunately, many students, almost 45% of Florida students, simply don't apply—leaving over *$100 million on the table ever year*. There are many reasons for this:

- Parents think they make too much or will not qualify
- Parents make mistakes on the form
- Parents do not know if the student is going to college or not, so they do not apply by the deadline
- Parents think it is too complicated of a process and not worth the hassle
- Parents think it will somehow hurt their business or child's chances of getting into a college

Just imagine $100 million sitting on a table and saying, "Nope—I don't want any part of that for a ten-minute application!" There is no reason not to complete your FAFSA. If applying for college, you should just do it. *Also, by not doing it, you could be excluded from other scholarship opportunities*!

To simplify everything, here are some key things to know about federal scholarships or FAFSA:

- FAFSA started opening earlier during the 2016-2017 school year with an October 1st date (prior it was January 1st).

- The FAFSA form is used to determine the amount of money a family is expected to contribute to the price of attending a postsecondary institution, called the EFC. The results of the FAFSA are used in determining student grants, work study, and loan amounts.

  - Grants = Free money. This money does not need to be repaid
  - Loans = Money you have to pay back. If you can avoid loans, do so.
  - Work Study = Working on campus provides the student spending money, but also some goes towards their tuition bill. There are some great work study opportunities for students, and the school works around student's schedules, plus they do not have leave campus.
  - When you accept the Award Letter, you can decide what type of Financial Aid you want to take, specifically the loans (always take grants!!) and work study.

---

[20] FCAN, 2013.

- Parents will use the prior-year tax return to complete FAFSA. So for seniors in 2017-2018, they will use their 2016 tax return.

- Every university uses their own formula to find the EFC amount, so while you may not qualify at one school, you might at another. The formula contains a lot of different components, and I often have families pleasantly surprised to receive money.

- FAFSA is given out like a big pile of money—the sooner a student applies, the more money they are likely to receive. A higher education institution only has so much financial aid to give, and once they have given it out in Award Letters, it is gone. The sooner the better.

- Admissions is not contingent on financial aid, as some universities used to do. Often admissions and the financial aid process are completely separate.

- FAFSA is not based on grades, extra-curriculars, or anything other than your FAFSA. This truly provides access to higher education that some students never thought they had.

FAFSA OPENS OCTOBER 1st
EVERYONE SHOULD COMPLETE IT!

LOCAL SCHOLARSHIPS

I LOVE local scholarships!! This is often an overlooked money resource for many families, simply because they do not know they exist. Unlike national scholarships, where hundreds of students may apply, local scholarships often see only a handful of applicants, sometimes only one or two! Those are great odds!

As well, local scholarships are created from local community members, organizations, and programs that believe in supporting students in their quest for higher education. Typically, local scholarships are managed by a community foundation that is separate from the school, and hold to what the original donor wanted, such as:

- Specific career or program paths (i.e., education, law, nursing, medicine)
- Specific universities or colleges
- Gender or ethnicity (i.e., female going into engineering, first generation student)
- Academic achievement
- Community service or involvement
- Extra-curriculars (i.e., sports, music)
- Organization where a parent works (i.e., electric company, real estate, education)
- Involvement in a special organization (i.e., Kiwanis, Rotary Club, Girl/Boy Scouts)

Things often needed to apply for a local scholarship:

- Application
- Recommendation letters
- Essay
- Transcript and/or standardized test scores (ACT/SAT)

In SW Florida, one of our local scholarship foundations is:

SW Florida Community Foundation

 floridacommunity.com/scholarships

OPENS early January, 2018
CLOSES early March, 2018

- They awarded $800,000 through 50 competitive scholarship funds.
- Scholarships awarded may be specific to local, in-state, or out-of-state colleges and universities. Students are often surprised by the variety.

> Ask your school counselor to find out more about these scholarship opportunities!

Florida County/Local Resources

Broward: Community Foundation of Broward:
http://cfbroward.org/scholarships

Charlotte: Charlotte Community Foundation
https://www.charlottecf.org/types-of-grants/scholarships/

Collier: Community Foundation of Collier County- http://www.cfcollier.org/students/

Collier: Collier County Public Schools
http://www.collierschools.com/scholarships

Eastern Florida: Eastern Florida Local Scholarships
http://www.easternflorida.edu/admissions/financial-aid-scholarships/scholarship-information/outside-scholarships.cfm

Hernando: Hernando County Education Foundation
https://www.hernandoeducationfoundation.org/p/61/student-scholarships#.WRnM6GjytPY

Hillsborough: Hillsborough Education Foundation
http://www.educationfoundation.com/scholarships

Indian River County: Scholarship Foundation of Indian River County
http://www.sfindianriver.org/

Northeast Florida: Community Foundation for Northeast Florida
https://www.jaxcf.org/file/2016/01/2015-TCF-Putnam-County-Grants.pdf

Ocala & Marion: Ocala Marion County Community Foundation
http://www.ocalafoundation.org/

Okaloosa: Okaloosa County School District
https://www.okaloosaschools.com/students/scholarships-local

Osceola: Osceola Education Foundation
https://www.foundationosceola.org/p/10/scholarships#.WRnOJ2jytPY

Palm Beach & Martin: Community Foundation for Palm Beach and Martin Counties
http://www.yourcommunityfoundation.org/

Polk: Polk Education Foundation Scholarships
http://www.polk-fl.net/students/collegeandcareer/financialaid/pefscholarships.htm

Sarasota: Community Foundation of Sarasota County
https://www.cfsarasota.org/Students/Students-Supporting-Your-Education

SW Florida: SW Florida Community Foundation
http://floridacommunity.com/scholarships/

STATE SCHOLARSHIPS

Florida offers several state scholarships that are available to a wide variety of students.

The Florida Department of Education, Office of Student Financial Assistance (OSFA), administers a variety of state-funded grants and scholarships to assist Florida residents with the cost of their postsecondary education.

Information can be found at:

 http://www.floridastudentfinancialaid.org/SSFAD/home/uamain.htm

Grants and Scholarship Programs Administered by OSFA

- Access to Better Learning and Education (ABLE) Grant

- Bright Futures Scholarship*

- First Generation Matching Grant

- Benacquisto Scholarship Program
  (formerly Florida Incentive Scholarship Program)

- Florida Fund for Minority Teachers

- Florida Resident Access Grant (FRAG)

- Florida Student Assistance Grant (FSAG)

- Florida Public Postsecondary Career Education
  Student Assistance Grant

- Florida Work Experience Program

- José Martí Scholarship Challenge Grant*

- Mary McLeod Bethune Scholarship

- Rosewood Family Scholarship*

- Scholarships for Children and Spouses of Deceased
  or Disabled Veterans*

Students *must* submit a completed Florida Financial Aid Application (FFAA)
to OSFA for programs denoted by an asterisk (*).

BRIGHT FUTURES

One of the most widely known state scholarships is called Florida Bright Futures Scholarship, which offers qualifying students approximately $1,800 to $6,000 worth of annual scholarships.

Bright Futures is a statewide scholarship program funded by the state government that was started in 1997, funded by the Florida Lottery. The eligibility has changed over the years, due to state funding, making the eligibility much higher than any prior years. There have been recent changes to funding, and the current hope (2017-2018 and beyond) is that the following funding levels continue.

For information please refer to this website:

 http://www.floridastudentfinancialaid.org/ssfad/bf/

Florida Academic Scholars	Florida Medallion Scholars
– 1290 SAT/ 29 ACT	– 1170 SAT/ 26 ACT
– 100 hours of community service	– 75 hours of community service
– 100% tuition + $300 book stipend	– $77 per credit hour

Gold Seal Vocational Scholars (GSV)	Gold Seal Cape Scholars (GSC)
– Used for career education or certificate programs	– Used for career education or certificate programs
– Meet general requirements for BF	– Meet general requirements for BF
– 30 hours of community service	– Used for career education or certificate programs
– ACT/SAT/PERT scores	– 30 hours of community service
– Weighted 3.0 GPA in non-elective courses	

IMPORTANT KEY THINGS TO KNOW ABOUT FAS & FMS SCHOLARSHIP

Qualifications: Many students qualify for the BF Scholarship, but do not realize it for several reasons:

GPA - Bright Futures uses a recalculated, weighted GPA that focuses on the core subject area (math, English, social sciences, mathematics, foreign language) and potentially fine arts, if needed. Students receive a .25 per semester course or .50 per year course in the calculation of the GPA in college-preparatory credit such as Honors, Pre-AICE, Pre=IB, and AP, IB, Dual-Enrollment.

ACT or **SAT** - Posted as needing composite score, but can actually be SuperScored (like GPA, they take highest score from any test sitting).

Community Service Hours - One part of scholarship program requires 75-100 community service hours, depending on the level of eligibility during their ninth through twelfth grade years. Students may exceed this amount of hours, and from a college admission standpoint should do more, but this is the requirement for this scholarship. The community service hours total is a four-year cumulative—not yearly.

Other ways to demonstrate academic merit is through programs such as National Merit Finalists & Scholarships, National Hispanic Scholars, AICE Diploma, and IB.

Applying

✓ Go to the website and fill out Florida Financial Aid Application (FFAA). That name is deceptive, because Bright Futures is *not* dependent on financial need—it is used primarily to collect student information.

✓ Ensure all criteria is met to submit community service hours (Lee County requires special documents be completed and given to the school). This is a great thing to talk to your school counselor about!

✓ Take the ACT and/or SAT until you receive the score needed (see the next chart).

✓ High Schools should send transcript and test scores according to their process.

✓ Inform Bright Futures where you are attending school.

APPLYING FOR SCHOLARSHIPS

You know what types of scholarships are out there, but here are some things to consider. I would *highly* suggest families talk about these key points to ensure a clear and direct communication about what is needed from both the student and the parents.

Things to Discuss:

HOW MUCH TIME DO I SPEND SEARCHING FOR SCHOLARSHIPS?

DO I HAVE MY DOCUMENTS TOGETHER?

WHAT ARE THE DEADLINES?

WHAT ARE MY FINANCIAL GOALS?

HOW CAN WE WORK TOGETHER AS A FAMILY TO EARN MORE SCHOLARSHIP MONEY?

As a student, write down some unique attributes about you (for example, sports, academic awards, heritage, programs, internships, or career interests). This will help you decide what you might qualify for in applying. If you do not meet the qualifications, such as going to an in-state school when you are going out-of-state, do not waste your time or the scholarship committee's time in applying.

My Unique Attributes Table

DOCUMENTS NEEDED FOR SCHOLARSHIPS

If you are ready with your application documents, it will make the whole process smoother and less stressful for everyone, as your scholarship documents are similar! Here are some things you will need to have in order.

NOTE: You may need to make changes for each scholarship, but if you have a solid beginning, it will definitely help.

- **Resume:** Just like applying for a job, you should have a resume of your high school career. Be sure this is well-edited and encapsulates everything you have done in high school. Have a parent or teacher go over this to ensure it is correct.

- **Essay:** I would suggest using some of the essays provided on Common Application to get you started, particularly the ones about your identity or background.

 www.commonapp.org

- **Recommendation Letters:** These are crucial in the scholarship process. You should request one from a school counselor, teacher, coach, or activity sponsor, and one from your personal life, such as a boss, pastor, or internship director. Give them a copy of your completed resume and ask them to talk about different things about you. For example, your teacher should talk about you as a student, whereas your coach would talk about you as a player. Having a variety of recommendations allows for you to be ready when the scholarship asks for a specific need. You don't need to use all of them, all the time, but it gives you more options!

I advise students not to send random scholarship links without notifying recommenders ahead of time. To be courteous, please inform them what the scholarship is for and the deadlines to submit. Some recommendations are quite lengthy, and if they are ill-prepared, the recommendation will not be as good.

SCHOLARSHIP CHECKLIST

Fill out some scholarships for which you are applying, so you can keep track. Feel free to reprint this page if you have more than the space allotted.

Type	Website	Deadline	Key Attributes	Documents Needed	Submitted

AWARD LETTERS

You have gone through the process of applying to these universities with the hopes that you will receive admissions to that college and scholarship opportunities.

Universities will first send an acceptance, deny, or deferred letter.

- If accepted, you will receive a letter/package in the mail. However, sometimes it shows up by email or institutional portal asking you to accept the offer and pick your room and board. You do not have to do this until May 1st, once you have received and reviewed all your financial aid. Usually your Award Letter comes *after* your admission decisions—sometimes months later.

- If deferred or denied, contact Admissions and see if there is a way for them to reconsider. Maybe a personal letter, recommendation, different starts date, or retesting on the ACT and SAT could gain you admissions. Sometimes, they also make mistakes, so it is best to check in with them. This is why it is important to know your Admission Rep!

What Is an Award Letter?

An award letter is the complete financial aid and scholarship package a student receives from a specific institution. The award letters are sent out via mail or email/institutional portal after admission to a university or college is given. No form is designated to use, so every institution creates their own. This is important to know as you compare packages.

What Does the Award Letter Include?

The award letter starts with the *Cost of Attendance* or *Sticker Price*, which includes an estimation of tuition, room and board, books, transportation, and fees. This price can go up or down, depending on what housing you pick (on or off campus), meal plans, and so forth. However, after scholarships and financial aid are distributed, you receive a *Net Price*.

There are also *Net Price Calculators* that colleges use to show you what to expect on your award letter, either here or on the school's website.

 https://professionals.collegeboard.org/higher-ed/financial-aid/netprice

Using the website Big Futures to calculate your family's *Expected Family Contribution* (EFC) can help you know what type of grant and loan money you could expect. Some of the following information shows you that a lot of families who think they DO NOT qualify, **DO** qualify.

 https://bigfuture.collegeboard.org/pay-for-college/paying-your-share/expected-family-contribution-calculator

Award letters come in varying styles. The award letter often includes federal and state grants and loans based on your EFC. Frequently they include state scholarships, like Bright Futures, and other institutional scholarships based on merit or specialized (You) scholarships. Not all award letters are the same. Some are very detailed, while others are not. If you are confused or need further explanation, it is best to talk with the college's Financial Aid Office. Some Admissions Representatives will sit down with you and go over exactly what each number and item means.

Traditionally, it is based on semester and annual enrollment. Scholarships and financial aid can increase or decrease with time, so it is best to understand the two- to four-year implications.

What Do I Do with My Award Letter?

You may either accept none, some, or your entire award letter:

- Students may not wish to attend that particular institution, so they would *deny* the award letter. It is not transferrable to other colleges, but you may talk with another Financial Aid Office to see if they can match or beat the award letter from another institution.
- You may accept *some* of the award letter, which often is the loans or work study program, but always accept grants, as it is *free* money!
- You may accept the *entire* award letter, which means you choose to attend that university and take the scholarships, grants, loans, and/or work study offered.

Sample Award Letters (SUS)

Here is a sample award letter from University of Florida:

Estimated Cost of Attendance from 08/22/2012 to 05/06/2013			$20,910.00
Minus:			
Expected Parental Contribution			$1,217.00
Expected Student/ Spouse Contribution			$231.00
Equals your gross financial need			$19,462.00

Award Detail	Fall	Spring	Total
Fed. Pell Grant	$2,050.00	$2,050.00	$4,100.00
Fed. Work-Study	$1,500.00	$1,500.00	$3,000.00
Fla. Student Assistance Grant	$1,206.00	$1,206.00	$2,412.00
FLa. Medallion Scholars Award	$1,140.00	$1,140.00	$2,280.00
Federal Loan	$3,612.00	$3,612.00	$7,224.00
Douglas Turner Grant	$223.00	$223.00	$446.00

What Does This Award Letter Mean?

Based on the family's FAFSA filing, the University of Florida came up with an EFC number that said the parents and student could pay around $1,500.00 of tuition every year. Because of the EFC number, the student received *several grants that do not need to be repaid*. The student also received the *FMS Bright Futures* scholarship which further reduced the cost.

The student also can agree to a work-study program where they would receive a job on campus, earn an hourly wage, but will have a decrease of tuition as well. Finally, the student will take on about $7,224.00 of loans every year, totaling around $29,000 at the end of four years. As well, the parents and student will need to cover the remaining ~$1,000 of attendance.

One question to ask is, are the loans subsidized or unsubsidized? This answer will let you know when the loans need to be paid back.

Sample Award Letter- PCUF

To show you a comparison of public versus private school, here is another award letter from Florida Southern College, a top-rated private college in Lakeland, Florida—with free application!

Award Detail	Fall	Spring	Total
Pfeiffer Scholarships	$6,500	$6,500	$13,000
Scholars Residency Grant-On Campus	$3,000	$3,000	$6,000
FSC Grant	$1,000	$1,000	$2,000
Federal PELL Grant	$1,885	$1,885	$3,770
Florida Student Assistance Grant	$650	$650	$1,300
Florida Resident Access Grant	$1,500	$1,500	$3,000
Bright Futures Academic Scholar	$1,648	$1,648	$3,296
Christoverson Scholarship	$1,000	$1,000	$2,000
Fed. Direct Loan Subsidized	$1,750	$1,750	$3,500
Fed. Direct Loan Unsubsidized	$1,000	$1,000	$2,000
Total Award	$19,933	$19,933	$39,866

The estimated tuition and fees for 2017-2018 year total $34,774. For residential students, the estimated cost for a double-occupany room and a full meal plan is $11,204.

What Does This Award Letter Mean?

Tuition, room, and board come in around $45,978, which is well over UF's tuition room and board of $20,190 (which has increased to over $22,000). However, let's break this down

	UF	FSC
Tuition, Room & Board	$20,190	$45,978
Grants & Scholarships	$12.238	$34,296
Loans	$7,224	$5,500
Total to Pay	$7.952.00	$11,682

In the end, even though FSC's sticker price is almost double UF's, it came close to a public university's net price. What is not listed is a work-study program through FSC. Adding that on, it could beat UF in price. These are all things to consider when looking at award letters!

These award letters are similar to what you will receive at any post-secondary institution. There are no rules regulating how it should be presented, but they are similar. It is very important when these are received to thoroughly analyze each package to be able to make the best decision possible.

Students will receive their award letters no later than May 1st, but usually several weeks or months before. If the student qualified for the Bright Futures FMS award, I would *highly* suggest signing up for the June ACT and/or SAT tests their senior year, as they would receive one more opportunity to earn the FAS level. With the new increased proposed FAS award amounts of 100% tuition + $300, it would be in the family and student's best interest to do *everything* they can to earn that top score.

CHAPTER 5
STAYING ON TRACK

Use this chapter to keep you on track with a detailed checklist, calendar, and online resources.

Chapter 4 is designed to walk you through what should happen after you apply to universities. This includes understanding the varying types of scholarships, as well as finalizing any decisions you may have.

Documents include:

- Checklists
- Glossary
- Organizational Tools
- Online Resources
- Calendar
- References

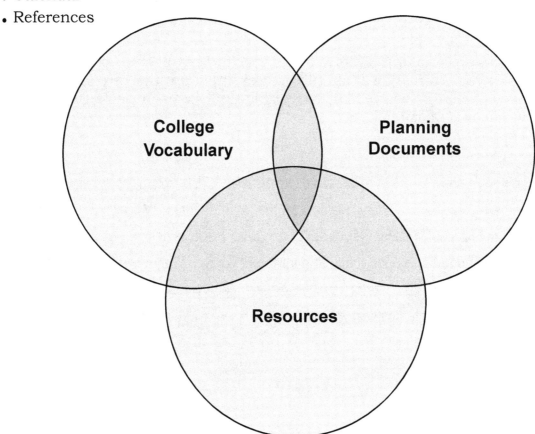

PREPARING FOR COLLEGE: CHECKLIST

9th-10th Grade

Fall	
	Explore the career and college readiness options at your school, local community, and through online programs.
	Create an Academic Plan in Chapter 1: "Creating an Academic Plan."
	Begin to strengthen your extra-curriculars and community service.
	Start developing a résumé, which is a record of your accomplishments, activities, and work experiences. This will be an important part of your college application.
	Create and build your Raise.Me account, adding information every semester.
	Meet with your school counselor to ensure you are on track each year.

11th Grade

Fall	
	Start your year off right by talking with your school counselor about the year ahead. Confirm that your courses will put you on the right track for college admission. Make sure that you will be enrolled in the most challenging courses for which you are qualified.
	Work on Chapter 1: "Creating an Academic Plan" in this Guidebook to know where you stand going into college admissions.
	Sign up for the PSAT at your school (October). This is great practice and can provide scholarship opportunities.
	Be sure to ask about test dates for the ACT and SAT. Register for the fall and spring offering of the SAT and/or ACT. You'll need to register up to six weeks ahead of time at www.actstudent.org or www.collegeboard.org. Ask your school counselor if you qualify for a fee waiver.
	Continue working on your résumé. Look for areas in which you can focus on to show your strengths and talents.
	If you haven't participated in many activities outside of class, now is the time to sign up. Consider clubs at schools, team sports, leadership roles, or involvement in your religious or civic community group.
	Line up a summer job, internship or co-op.
	Begin taking a more serious look at colleges and universities. Make a file for each college and gather information about academics, financial aid, and campus life. Go to college fairs and open houses and learn as much as you can about the colleges online.
	Begin planning college visits. Try to visit colleges near you and include a large, medium-size, and small campus.
	Develop a preliminary list of colleges that interest you.

11th *Grade Spring*

	Begin Chapter 2 & 3 in this Guidebook.
	Take a look at some college applications and consider all of the different pieces of information you will need to compile. Practice college essays. Having a good sense of what colleges ask and how to write a good essay will ease the process for later.
	Make a list of teachers, counselors, employers, and other adults you might ask to write letters of recommendation for your college applications. Fill out the Counselor Recommendation Questionnaire, Teacher Recommendation Form, and build your resume.
	Continue with formal and informal college visits.
	Begin talking to college admission representatives for each college
	Sign up for the ACT/SAT. Use the resources provided in Chapter 1 to study. View this as your last test, and aim for the highest score possible.

11th *Grade Summer*

	Begin Chapter 3 & Chapter 4: "College Applications & Scholarships."
	Continue investigating colleges. On-campus college visits, both formal and informal visits are crucial.
	Thoroughly edit and complete your resume- volunteer opportunities, internships, research, etc.
	Write, edit, and complete your college essays. Have them reviewed by trusted adults and your school counselor.
	Begin researching about your applications. Generally, colleges will have their applications online by the beginning of July or August.
	Begin researching scholarships, build your www.raise.me account, and explore www.fastweb.com and other scholarship websites, such as the Scholly App. Dedicate one to two hours every week to scholarship searching, as the payoff can be substantial.

12th *Grade* — August/September

	Register for the SAT and/or ACT if you didn't take it as a junior, or if you aren't satisfied with your score and want to take it again.
	Take a look at some college applications and consider all of the different pieces of information you will need to compile. Request unofficial transcript to help fill out information and copy of current schedule.
	Visit with your school counselor to make sure you are on track to fulfill all requirements for high school graduation and college admission requirements.
	Take every opportunity to get to know colleges: meeting with college representatives who visit your high schools during the fall, attending local college fairs, and visiting campuses. Many schools have on-campus, special campus visitation programs—great opportunity to get the feel of the college.
	Narrow down your list of colleges and begin to consider Reach, Just Right, or Safety schools. Make sure you have the application and financial aid information for each school. Find out if you qualify for any scholarships at these schools and what you need to do to apply for them.

	Utilize the checklist and calendar in the Guidebook to keep track of: • Standardized test dates, registration deadlines, and fees • College application due dates • Financial aid application forms and deadlines • Other materials you'll need for college applications (recommendations, transcripts, essays, etc.) • Your high school's application processing deadlines Some schools require the CSS/Financial Aid Profile. Ask the colleges to which you are applying for their deadlines. Register as early as September. If you used fee waivers for the ACT and/or SAT, see your counselor about application fee waivers.
	Request personal recommendations from your school counselors, teachers, coaches, and/or sometimes a "personal" reference. Follow the process listed in this workbook as each school and application is different. Be sure to provide the appropriate college forms (Common App form), an outline of your resume, and College Recommendation Form to each person writing you a recommendation. Allow approximately three to four weeks for each teacher to complete.

— October

	Some colleges will have deadlines as early as this month. These would include Rolling Admission, Early Decision, and Early Action deadlines.
	If you cannot afford the application fees that many colleges charge, ask your school counselor to help you request a fee waiver.
	Continue researching scholarships. Investigate college, religious, and civic groups for scholarship opportunities. There are also some good scholarship websites, including FastWeb (www.fastweb.com) and The College Board (http://bigfuture.collegeboard.org/scholarship-search). You should NEVER pay for scholarship information.
	The FAFSA (Free Application for Federal Student Aid) has moved to October 1st! Complete your FAFSA forms as soon as you possibly can. Visit www.fafsa.gov to complete this form. The sooner you complete it, the sooner you will have an idea of your financial aid options. Watch the mail for your Student Aid Report (SAR)—it should arrive four weeks after the FAFSA is filed or watch your email if you filed electronically. Even if you think you do not qualify, colleges and scholarships need the information. Many scholarships are connected to it, so by not filling it out, you are eliminating a substantial amount of free money.
	Fill out the Florida Financial Aid Application (FFAA) this month to be eligible for state scholarships.
	Most Priority Deadlines for the SUS and PCUF are November 1st. By applying by this date, there are greater chances for admissions and scholarships. I suggest every student strive to meet this deadline!

— November

	Finalize and send any early decision or early action applications due this month. Have a parent, teacher, or your school counselor, or other adult review the application before it is submitted—NO typos!!!
	Every college will require a copy of your transcript from your high school. Follow your school's procedure for sending transcripts.
	Make sure testing companies (ACT or SAT) have sent your scores directly to the colleges to which you are applying.
	Do a graduation credit check with your school counselor for Spring Semester 2. Do you have ALL the courses necessary to graduate?
	Review transcript for any issues.
	Finish Chapter 4

December

	Begin to organize regular decision applications and financial aid forms, which will be due in January and/or February.
	Register for the January SAT (if needed). It is the last one colleges will be able to consider for a senior.
	Several universities, like UF, require the application first, then all remaining documents. Be sure all information is given by the college's deadlines, typically in December.
	If you haven't asked for your recommenders to write a recommendation for scholarships (a bit different than a college application recommendation), be sure you do so. Give them time and a small token of appreciation! Be sure you save multiple copies to send to numerous scholarships.
	Check with how many community service hours you have currently in the school's system for Bright Futures. If missing hours, be sure to organize some volunteer and community service work.

January

	Many popular and selective colleges will have application deadlines as early as January 1. Others have deadlines later in January and February. Keep track of and observe deadlines for sending in all required fees and paperwork.
	If necessary, register for the February ACT (some colleges will be able consider it). This might be also used for Bright Futures (Florida resident scholarships) if you need the scores to receive it.
	Ask in January to send first semester transcripts to schools where you applied. At the end of the school year, they will need to send final transcripts to the college you will attend.
	While most of your applications are complete and you are waiting to receive admission decisions, don't slack in the classroom. The college that you do attend will want to see your second semester transcript. No Senioritis!
	Several local scholarships open this month. Be sure to ask your counselor about these crucial scholarship opportunities, organize all your documents needed, and contact the individual foundations to ensure all materials have been submitted.

March/April

	Acceptance letters and financial aid offers will start to arrive. Review your acceptances, compare financial aid packages, and visit your final choices, especially if you haven't already.
	During this time, there will be quite a few things your high school will ask you to do. Often times there are meetings about graduation, documents such as a Senior Questionnaire/Survey, grad checks for all classes, and so forth. All meetings are crucial!
	Fill out Bright Futures (Florida residents). Be sure your school has all your community service hours (75-100) in the computer system.

May

	May 1 is the date when the college you plan to attend requires a commitment and deposit. When you've made your college decision, notify your school counselor and the colleges. Send in your deposit by the postmark date of May 1. If you've been offered financial aid, accept the offer and follow the instructions given. Also notify schools you will *not* attend of your decision.
	Make sure that you have requested that your final transcript be sent to the school you will be attending.
	If you are "wait listed" by a college you really want to attend, visit, call and write the admission office to make your interest clear. Ask how you can strengthen your application. GRADUATE!!

GLOSSARY OF TERMS

Terminology: High School Programs

Academic Core: These include all courses taken in English, social studies, mathematics, sciences, and foreign language.

Academic Electives: This is sort of a gray area in college admissions. These are courses that students elected to take, but are more academic (i.e., psychology, human geography, or speech). Typically, these courses are included in the recalculation.

Advanced Placement (AP): AP courses are college-level classes taught in high school, following guidelines and covering material that should prepare them to take Advanced Placement tests offered by the College Board. AP courses have a final AP exam that students need to take. College credit is dependent on the score of the exam and the university they are attending.

Advanced Standing Credit: Credit for previously completed college-level work or demonstrated knowledge of a subject granted by taking advanced standing exams, such as advanced placement (AP) or international baccalaureate (IB) exams, and other similar programs.

Cambridge AICE Diploma: The Cambridge Advanced International Certificate for Education (AICE) is an international curriculum and examination system that emphasizes the value of broad and balanced study. Students take courses in math, sciences, languages, and arts and humanities. Students sit for exams that could earn them college credit, if passed.

Career & Technical Certificate: Programs for high school students that provide career and technical instruction consisting of technical skills in workforce areas, including agriculture, architecture, arts and AV, business, education, health, IT, manufacturing, and public safety. The programs may be on or off the school campus.

College-Level Examination Program (CLEP): The CLEP is a set of tests that can be administered to students who desire to obtain college credit by taking proficiency tests in selected courses. If the student scores high enough on the test, college credit can be awarded. There is a charge for each test taken. Information concerning an individual institution's policies toward CLEP Tests can be found in the institution's catalog.

Dual Enrollment: A process allowing high school students to take college-level courses that can be transferred to a college or university for credit. It may also be called Concurrent Enrollment. The credits may be available both for college and high school credits. Different requirements exist for taking dual-enrollment, like a specific grade point average or standardized test scores.

Early College High School: Early College is a high school program that combines the high school curriculum with the first two years of college. When students finish early college high school, they have a high school diploma and possibly an associate's degree or two year's equivalent of college credit to transfer to a four-year college. This approach especially targets students who will be first in their family to attend college, and/or of lower income means, as it makes earning college credits more affordable and accessible.

Electives: Electives are courses that do not fall in the core courses. These include classes like PE, computer, business, arts, and study hall.

GPA (Grade Point Average): Quantitative measure of a student's grades. The GPA is figured by averaging the numerical value of a student's grades. It is cumulative, starting freshman year—grades count every year. A poor GPA in ninth grade can drag down the overall average, despite, for example, good grades junior year. Some schools "weight" their GPAs by adding points to more rigorous courses like honors and college-level courses.

Unweighted: this simply means the student does not receive any extra points for more rigorous courses like honors, dual enrollment, or Advanced Placement. An A in PE would be the same as an A in AP Human Geography.

Weighted: this GPA takes into account a student's rigor of coursework. More points are awarded for more rigorous courses—the more rigor, the more points. Student class rankings are often determined off this.

High School Graduation Requirements: High school graduation requirements are the classes (or units) needed to receive a high school diploma. Every state has different requirements so it is important you are not missing any requirements or you are not able to receive a standardized diploma.

International Baccalaureate (IB): The International Baccalaureate program provides participating high schools a challenging academic course load and additional learning projects. The IB program lasts two years and requires students to study six subjects chosen from the six subject groups: language acquisition, experimental sciences, language and literature, individuals and societies, mathematics and computer sciences, the arts, complete an extended essay, take a theory of knowledge course, or participate in "creativity, action, or service."

National Honor Society: National Honor Society is an organization at participating high schools that recognizes students for academics, service, leadership and character. Each Honor Society chapter establishes rules for membership that are based upon a student's outstanding performance in the areas of: scholarship, service, leadership, and character. Students in grades 10 through 12 in a school with both an official charter of the National Honor Society and an active affiliation with the national office are eligible for consideration for membership in NHS.

PLAN Test: This test is usually taken in the sophomore year to prepare the student for the ACT.

PSAT: PSAT is shorthand for Preliminary Scholastic Assessment Test. This standardized test is practice for the SAT and covers reading, math and writing. It is typically taken during a student's sophomore or junior years (grades 10 or 11). This test is offered for a fee at high schools. A fee waiver is often available for students from low-income families. The PSAT also qualifies the 50,000 top scoring students across the United States for the National Merit Scholarship.

Resume: A high school resume provides a snapshot of a student's accomplishments, extracurriculars, hobbies, and work history. They are a useful tool for prepping for a college interview, giving to teachers to write letters of recommendation, and filling out college applications.

TERMINOLOGY: THE ADMISSIONS PROCESS

ACT: A two-hour-and-55-minute examination that measures a student's knowledge and achievement in four subject areas (English, mathematics, reading, and science reasoning) to determine the student's readiness for college-level instruction. There is also an optional writing test that assesses students' skills in writing an essay. The ACT is scored on a scale of 1 to 36 for each of the four areas. The four subject area scores are averaged to create a Composite Score.

Admission: Admission is the act of being accepted into a post-secondary institution. After the application process to a post-secondary institution, the admissions office at the institution will notify the student by phone, mail or email of whether or not the student has been admitted. Admission to a postsecondary institution does not mean the student is required to go there, and does not mean the student is automatically enrolled. Admission is simply the acceptance of a student into the institution.

Application Deadline: The date set by college admissions when applications are due. If deadlines are missed, students will usually be denied or lose valuable opportunity for scholarships.

Campus Visit/Tour: A service by the college admissions office for prospective students, allowing them to visit various campus buildings, meet key institutional personnel, and get a firsthand look at campus life.

College Entrance Exams: The ACT and SAT are national exams that students must take to be admitted to most colleges and universities. Both tests are designed to measure a student's level of knowledge in basic areas, such as Math, English, Reading, and Science. It is recommended students take both the ACT and SAT. It is best to take at least one test during the junior year. Students may retest either test and should do so at the start of the senior year. The SAT II Subject area test is also required by some colleges and universities whose admission standards are more select. Visit 🔗 www.actstudent.org and 🔗 www.collegeboard.com for more information and registration.

Some schools use tests such as ACCUPLACER and PERT. Typically these are two-year community colleges that will take these or the ACT/SAT

College Essay: A brief composition on a single subject, required by many colleges as part of the application process for admission.

College Fair: An event at which colleges, universities, and other organizations related to higher education present themselves in an exposition atmosphere for the purpose of attracting and identifying potential applicants.

College Rep Visit: This is when a college or university admissions representative visits a high school or community site for the purpose of recruiting students for admission to the institution.

Common Application: A general application accepted by 700 colleges and universities throughout the United States and abroad (🔗 www.commonapp.org).

Coalition Application: A college application for over 90 universities and colleges dedicated to diversity and affordability (http://www.coalitionforcollegeaccess.org).

Deferred Admission: This is a college's option to postpone making a decision on whether to accept or deny an applicant. If deferred, they may be waiting for additional information from the student, like end of semester 1 grades for seniors, or to move you from one type of admission (early) to another (regular).

Deferred Enrollment: An accepted student's decision to put off a college's offer of admission in order to take a one-year absence (e.g., to travel, work, or take care of a family member).

Demonstrated Interest: This includes a student's expression of his or her desire to attend a particular college through campus visits, contact with admissions officers, and other actions that attract the attention of college admissions personnel. While not all institutions use this as a factor in accepting students for admissions, studies have shown that more than half of schools do consider demonstrated interest in their admissions decisions.

Early Action: A process that allows students to apply to a school earlier than normal (often before November) in order to receive an earlier decision (usually by mid-December). Students are allowed to apply to other schools as well, but they typically need to let the accepting colleges know by late spring if they'll be attending. With early action, you don't have to accept an offer of admission.

Early Decision: A process that allows students to apply to ONE college or university with the promise to attend if accepted. Early decision is binding, so students should be sure it's the school they want to (and can afford to) attend before applying early decision.

Essay: A written writing prompt that demonstrates a student's interest or best qualities that makes a student stand out in the application process.

Fee Waiver: Students with financial need may receive fee waivers to take the SAT, SAT II, and the ACT. Students who take the test using a fee waiver may then receive college application fee waivers.

First Generation College Student: Any student whose parents did not obtain a Bachelor's degree or higher at a U.S. accredited institution. It is up to the individual institutions to evaluate any Bachelor's degree or higher obtained from outside of the U.S.

Fit: The college search is not about getting into the best college. There is no school that is best for all students. Some students do best at large public universities; others excel in small liberal arts colleges; still others want to study far from home. If you want to make the most of college, don't just apply to the big–name schools or the ones your friends are excited about. Do your own research to find schools that are the best fit for you.

Institutional Application: The individual college has its own application, typically found online.

Interview: This is a personal, face-to-face interaction between an admissions applicant and an institutional representative (admissions officer, alumnus, faculty, etc.). Interviews are rarely required, but at colleges that offer them it can be beneficial to take advantage of the opportunity.

Just Right School: A just right school is where a student's high school grade point average, standardized test scores, and other factors match what the institution's admission criteria are. While not a guarantee, students have a good chance of admission.

Non-resident: A student who is not an official resident of the state where a public university is located. Tuition at public universities is less expensive for residents.

Open Admission: A policy of some colleges of admitting all high school graduates, regardless of academic qualifications, such as high school grades and admission test scores.

Personal Statement: An application essay in which a student gives more insight into his/her personality, achievements, history and character.

Reach School: A college or university that you have a chance of getting into, but your test scores, GPA and/or class rank are a bit on the low side when you look at the school's profile. The top U.S. colleges and top universities should always be considered Reach schools.

Recalculated GPA: A recalculated GPA is weighted of core content courses such as mathematics, science, social studies, English, and foreign language, and academic electives. It also gives extra weight to honors and college-level coursework. Electives are not included.

Recommendation: A letter written or institutional form on your behalf, explaining why you make a good candidate. Most applications require two to three recommendation letters and include teachers, counselors, or school administrators.

Regular Decision: The application period in which a student applies that does not have any binding or non-binding agreement attached to it.

Resident: A student who lives in and meets the residency requirements for the state where a public university is located. Tuition at public universities often is more expensive for non-residents.

Rolling Admissions: This is a process of reviewing and making decisions on applications as they are received, rather than according to a specific deadline.

Safety School: A college or university where you clearly meet the admission requirements, such as minimum GPA or test scores. It's important though that the school also be one that you would want to attend should you not gain admission to more selective colleges.

SAT: SAT is shorthand for the Scholastic Assessment Test. The SAT is a standardized test which may be used for admission into post-secondary institutions. It tests knowledge in writing, critical reading, and math. The exam is typically taken in the spring of a student's junior year, and can be retaken beginning in fall of senior year of high school as a student works to increase his/her score.

School Profile: This is an overview of your high school's program, grading system, course offerings, and other features that your school submits to Admissions Offices along with your transcript. For better or worse, admissions offices use this information to weigh your GPA, placing a student's GPA against the academic reputation of the school she or he attends.

SSAR: The Student Self-Reported Academic Record has students input their transcript into a system that recalculates the GPAs based on a college's criteria.

Transcript: An official academic record from a specific school, typically your high school or post-secondary institution. It lists the courses you have completed, grades and information such as when you attended.

Wait List: A list of college applicants who haven't been accepted or denied. If openings develop, the college may offer admission to some of the students on the wait list.

Waiver: Students who meet financial qualifications can receive fee waivers for the application.

TERMINOLOGY: COLLEGE PROGRAMS

2 + 2 Program: 2 + 2 students complete their first two years (60 credits or Associates degree) at a two-year state college or community college and complete their last two years at a four-year institution. Some colleges and universities have matriculation agreements among themselves, meaning if you do the first two years at College X, College Y will accept you.

Art School (Arts College, Art Institute, Conservatory): An institution specializing in the visual, performing, and/or creative arts.

Associate's Degree: A type of degree awarded to students at a US community college, usually after two years of classes. An associate's degree can be earned at two-year and some four-year post-secondary institutions. The hours of credit required vary by the program of study, but it typically is the equivalent to four semesters of full-time study, or approximately 60 credit hours.

Associates of Art (AA): A two-year "common core" degree that includes math, science, humanities, communication, social science (~36 credits), and electives (~24 credits). Students seeking an AA degree typically go on to a four-year university.

Associates of Science (AS): An A.S. degree is best suited for students that want to enter a career field after two years, but want the option to transfer to a four-year college in a related field. It requires less core coursework than an A.A., and is more specific to particular major or career path.

Bachelor's Degree: A degree awarded to undergraduates, usually after four years of college classes. Bachelor's degree programs typically take four to five years of college-level coursework, and require approximately 120 credit hours to complete. A bachelor's degree is awarded to students who fulfill the requirements set by the post-secondary institution. Credentials commonly associated with a bachelor's degree are bachelor of science (BS), and bachelor of arts (BA).

Certificate Program: A Certificate program teaches a specific skill set, and allows students to pursue a specialized area through specific training. Certificate programs may be offered at community colleges, technical/vocational schools, or proprietary schools. The length of training varies from 18-47 credit hours on the type of certificate sought.

College: A college is a common name for post-secondary institutions specifically in reference to institutions that award associate or bachelor degrees. It may also refer to those post-secondary institutions that only service undergraduate degrees and do not have graduate programs. In addition, within some undergraduate programs, colleges may refer to an area of study or program, such as the College of Pharmacy or College of Nursing.

Colleges That Change Lives: A program that consists of 40 colleges that are dedicated to the advancement and support of a student-centered colleges. These colleges have a goal of each student developing a lifelong love of learning and provide the foundation for a successful and fulfilling life beyond college.

Four-Year College/University: Four-year colleges and universities are post-secondary institutions that award bachelor's degrees to those who complete the required coursework. Four-year post-secondary institutions can be for profit, not for profit, public, or private.

Gap-Year Programs: Year-long programs designed for high school graduates who wish to defer enrollment in college while engaging in meaningful activities, such as academic programs, structured travel, or community service.

Historically Black College: Historically black colleges and universities (HBCUs) are institutions of higher education in the United States that were established before 1964 with the intention of serving the black community. They operate the following websites:

- www.firstinthefamily.org
- www.whatkidscando.org
- info@firstinthefamily.org

There are 105 HBCUs today, including public and private, two-year and four-year institutions, medical schools, and community colleges. Almost all are in former slave states.

Ivy League: Eight colleges are considered Ivy League, because of their selectivity, high rigor, and prestige. They are often ranked as some of the best colleges in the world, with top access to resources, research, and academic programs.

Liberal Arts College: Liberal Arts colleges are post-secondary institutions whose curriculum emphasizes broad general knowledge of humanities, and social and physical sciences, rather than focusing on a narrow issue or profession (like nursing or social work). Liberal arts colleges tend to be smaller in size.

Post-Secondary Education: Post-secondary education refers to formal education beyond high school. Post-secondary education institutions include: colleges, universities, technical schools, and vocational training centers. The lengths of these programs vary, and upon completion of the desired program, one may earn a certificate or degree.

Private University: A university that is privately-funded. Tuition for a private college or university (before scholarships and grants) is the same for all students.

Public University: A university that is funded by the government. Public colleges and universities are less expensive for residents of the state where they are located.

Religion-Based Institution: These are colleges and universities established by and currently operating under the sponsorship of a church, synagogue, mosque, a denomination, or a particular religion.

Selectivity: Selectivity is the degree to which a college or university admits or denies admission based on the individual student's record of academic achievement. In general, a highly selective school admits 25% of applicants, a very selective school admits 26% to 49% of applicants, a selective school admits 50% to 75% of applicants and a school with open admission admits applicants based on space availability.

Single-Sex (or Single-Gender) College: This is a college that accepts either women only or men only.

Transfer Student: A transfer student is someone who has completed their first two years of college at one college, and then goes to another college to finish their degree. Typically, this term is used for students going from a community college with an AA or AS to a four-year university.

Two-Year College/Community College: Two-year colleges and community colleges are public post-secondary institutions. Students who complete the required coursework in their respective programs are awarded an associate's degree or certificate. Credits gained at these institutions are designed to transfer to four year colleges and universities, if desired.

Vocational or Technical School: A technical or vocational school is a post-secondary institution that provides specialized training in a career field. Programs offered teach a specific skill rather than traditional academic courses such as English and history. Technical schools often offer associates degree and certificate programs in careers ranging from carpentry to information technology.

TERMINOLOGY: COLLEGE PROGRAMS & ON-CAMPUS

Academic Year: The school year that begins with autumn classes. The academic year at most US colleges and universities starts in August or September.

Advisor: School official, usually assigned by your college or university, who can help choose your classes and make sure you are taking the right courses to graduate.

Attrition Rates: Many students start programs but change or drop out. This is known as the attrition rates. Knowing a program's attrition rates points to two things: 1) the program is rigorous and many students do not fully understand its coursework demands (as typical in engineering and medicine) or 2) the program is not well designed or poorly run, or presents other barriers to students. Combine a program's placement rate with attrition rate to paint a picture of the type of program it is.

Audit: To attend a class without receiving academic credit.

Course Number: The number your college or university uses to classify a course. You usually need this number in order to register for a class.

Credit Hour: The number of hours assigned to a specific class. This is usually the number of hours per week you are in the class. The number of credit hours you enroll in determines whether you are a full-time student or a part-time student.

Dean: Deans are the head of a specific department or program at post-secondary institutions. Deans are commonly former professors who oversee the faculty and students involved in those programs and, if necessary, are involved in the program's accreditation process.

Doctorate: Highest academic degree, awarded after a bachelor's degree or master's degree, depending on the needs of each program.

Elective: A class you can take that is not specifically required by your major or minor. These are generally courses you take for fun or just to see if something sparks your interest. Examples might include a theater class, a beginner's Spanish class, or volleyball.

Extracurricular activities: Groups you belong to outside of class, such as sporting teams, clubs, and organizations.

Fees: Fees are costs that are not part of tuition payments at post-secondary institutions. Fees may be charged in addition to tuition to cover the cost of student activities, facilities, or programs.

Freshman: First-year college student.

Full-time student: A student who enrolls in at least a minimum number (determined by your college or university) of credit hours of courses.

General education classes: Classes that give students basic knowledge of a variety of topics. Students often must take general education classes in order to graduate. This set of classes includes different courses and is called by assorted names at various colleges and universities.

Grade point average: The average of all of the course grades you have received, on a four-point scale.

Greek: Fraternities and sororities. They often have specific student housing options for their members.

Honors: An honors program at post-secondary institutions allows students with high academic achievement to be placed in courses designed to help students thoroughly explore topics and further develop critical thinking skills. Honors classes typically have a smaller class size and offer extra-curricular activities. Admission requirements of honors programs vary by institution, but typically place a standard on the SAT or ACT, high school class ranking or GPA, and a type of formal application procedure.

Internship: A temporary job, paid or unpaid, usually in the field of your major. You may be able to receive college credit for an internship.

Junior: Third-year college student.

Major: Your primary area of study. Your college major is the field you plan to get a job in after you graduate (for example: business, linguistics, anthropology, or psychology).

Master's degree: A degree awarded to graduate students. The awarding of a master's degree requires at least one year of study (and often more, depending on the field) after a student earns a bachelor's degree.

Minor: Your secondary area of study. Fewer classes are required for a college minor than for a major. Colleges and universities usually don't require students to have a minor. Many students' minors are a specialization of their major field. For example, students who want to become a science reporter might major in journalism and minor in biology.

Office hours: Time set aside by professors or teaching assistants for students to visit their office and ask questions or discuss the course they teach. Your professor or teaching assistant will tell you at the beginning of the term when and where office hours will be every week.

Online classes: Courses you take by computer instead of in a traditional classroom.

Part-time student: A student who doesn't enroll in enough credit hours to become a full-time student, as defined by your college or university. Part-time students often take only one or two classes at one time.

Placement Rates: When determining college programs, knowing their placement rates is crucial. Placement rates reflect the number of students from that program that either went on to graduate school or found a job in their field. The higher the placement rates, the more likely it is that the college has a strong program.

Placement Tests: Colleges and universities use these examinations to place students in courses—most often mathematics and foreign languages—that match their proficiency. In some cases, a student's level of competency on the test may exempt them from having to take a course required for graduation (see CLEP).

Prerequisite: A class that must be taken before you can take a different class. (For example, Astronomy 100 may be a prerequisite for Astronomy 200.)

Quarter: Type of academic term. A school with this system generally will have a fall quarter, winter quarter, and spring quarter (each about ten weeks long), along with a summer term (see also Semester).

RA: Short for resident assistant or resident adviser, an RA is a college student who supervises the other students living in a college dorm, usually in exchange for food and housing from the school.

Registrar: The registrar is an administrative department at a post-secondary institution, which maintains student academic records. These records include transcripts, degree completion status, and verification of enrollment and degrees.

Remediation: Remediation involves taking prerequisite classes, which are required for students prior to enrolling in an entry-level class in a subject area. A student who does not perform adequately on a section of a college entrance exam may be required to take a remedial class that is not for credit before enrolling in credit-bearing courses. Common remedial courses include English, math, and writing.

Semester: Type of academic term. A school with this system generally will have a fall semester and a spring semester (each about 15 weeks long), along with a summer term (see also, Quarter).

Senior: Fourth-year college student. You are a senior when you graduate from college.

Sophomore: Second-year college student.

Syllabus: A description of a course that also lists the dates of major exams, assignments, and projects.

Term: The length of time that you take a college class (see also, Quarter and Semester).

TERMINOLOGY: FINANCIAL AID & SCHOLARSHIPS

Athletic Scholarships: These scholarships are based upon athletic ability and your prospective college's departmental needs. Division I, II, and III college athletic scholarships are very difficult to receive, because of fierce competition.

Award Letter: An explanation of the financial aid a college will give a student, which may include grants, scholarships, student loans, and work-study.

Corporate Scholarships: These scholarships are awarded to help employees and their families, show community support, and to encourage future job seekers toward a career in the company's area of business. Corporate scholarships are much less competitive than other types of scholarships, because of geography, employment, and the relatively low number of applicants. Start with your family's employers and then check out the newspaper to see which companies in your area are awarding scholarships. Finally, contact these businesses to find out how to apply.

Expected Family Contribution (EFC): Expected Family Contribution is the amount of financial contribution a family is expected to pay towards the cost of college. This amount is based on a federal formula, and determines the student's eligibility for need-based financial aid. The EFC appears on a Student Aid Report (SAR), which is received after a student's FAFSA is processed.

Florida Financial Aid Application (FFAA): A form that is specific to Florida students that must be filled out in order to be eligible for any Florida state scholarships, such as Bright Futures scholarships.

Free Application for Federal Student Aid (FAFSA): A form that all students must fill out to be considered for federal financial aid.

Financial Aid: Money you receive for your college tuition or expenses that you may or may not have to pay back (see Grant, Loan, and Scholarship).

Full Cost of Attendance or "Sticker Price": The full cost of attendance refers to all expenses relevant to attending a particular postsecondary institution. This estimate is provided by the institution and includes tuition, fees, books, supplies, room and board, transportation, and personal expenses and is different for each institution.

Grant: A form of financial aid from a non-profit organization (such as the government) that you do not have to repay.

Institutional Scholarships: These scholarships are awarded by the college or university to reduce the cost of attending. Often these scholarships will be based upon extracurricular involvement, academics (see merit scholarship), student demographics, or other criteria. Upon admission, student's application will be reviewed for different scholarships, some automatically applied, while others are to be applied to.

Interest Bearing Loans: Interest bearing loans have an attached interest rate which will have to be repaid in addition to the amount of the loan. Interest is a fee charged to use the money. Interest rates are the rates charged to borrow the funds from an institution. Interest rates on loans can be fixed (will remain at the same initial rate) or adjusting (potentially increasing) over time.

Loan: A form of financial aid that you must repay. Loans are an amount of money provided to an individual on the terms that the money and gained interest will be repaid in full. Loans can be offered by the federal government, or by private institutions such as banks or other financial institutions. There are two types of federal loans: subsidized and unsubsidized (see definitions for each). These loans can have a fixed interest rate, adjusting, or (in rare cases) are interest free. Loans may be taken out by one individual or co-signed where more than one individual is responsible for the repayment of the loan.

Local Scholarships: Local scholarships typically come from the community in which the student resides. Usually there is an application process, each having differing criteria. Since these are normally smaller in denominations, students can often win multiple awards, as there are fewer applicants.

Micro-Scholarships: Becoming more popular, students can begin entering in their resume to start accruing smaller denominations for their work in high school. Micro-scholarships allow students to see their potential scholarship upfront before they apply.

Merit Aid: Financial aid that is awarded based on a student's achievements and/or talents (for example, academic or athletic).

National Scholarships: There are a tremendous amount of scholarship sites out there with large organizations giving away money. Typically these scholarships are larger in denomination, but more students are applying.

Need-Based Aid: Financial aid that is awarded based upon a student's ability to pay for college.

Need-Blind Admission: Full consideration of an applicant and his or her application without regard to the individual's need for financial aid.

Net-Price: Price of attendance, including tuition, room and board, books, transportation, and fees, minus scholarships and financial aid. Cost of attendance calculators, sometimes referred to as net price calculators, can be often be found on institution's website.

Pell-eligible: A "Pell-eligible" student is eligible to receive a Pell grant, which is a need-based grant provided by the federal government. To be Pell-eligible, students must fill out the Free Application for Federal Student Aid (FAFSA) and be seeking their first post-secondary degree. The amount of the award depends on the student's expected family contribution (EFC), cost of attendance, enrollment status (full or part time), and if the student will attend for a full academic year or less.

Pell Grant: Pell grants are awarded by the Federal Government to students who demonstrate financial need. Only students who are pursuing their first degree are eligible for Pell Grants. Recipients can study at any approved post-secondary institutions, which are then responsible for distributing the grant.

Private Loan: A private loan is from a financial institution other than the federal government, such as a bank or other financial institution. Private loans are typically unsubsidized loans and can either have a fixed interest rate (will remain at the same initial rate) or will be adjusting (potentially increasing) over time. Private loans typically have a higher interest rate than those offered by the federal government.

Private Organization Scholarships: These scholarship opportunities number in the millions. Places of worship, labor unions, school districts, chambers of commerce, and philanthropic organizations are all excellent sources for college scholarships. Sit down with your family and make a scholarship search list of potential sources.

Room and Board: Room and board is a typical name for the cost associated with living in on-campus housing and participating in a meal plan offered by the post-secondary institution.

Scholarship: A form of financial aid that you do not have to repay.

Subsidized Loans: Subsidized loans accrue over a student's time while in college with payment beginning six months after graduation. The federal government pays the interest for Direct Subsidized Loans while the student is in college or while the loan is in deferment. It is recommended that *IF* a loan is absolutely necessary, a subsidized loan should be the loan of preference.

Tuition: Tuition is the cost of the academic program at a post-secondary institution. Tuition is generally charged per credit hour. It varies for each post-secondary institution, and may vary depending on a student's residency status and level of coursework.

Unsubsidized Loans: Interest begins accruing for Direct Unsubsidized Loans as soon as the loan is taken out.

Work Study: A job (typically on campus) that allows a student to earn money to help pay for the costs associated with college.

COLLEGE PLANNING ORGANIZATIONAL TOOL

User Names & Passwords

Use this chart to write down all of your usernames and passwords you need to remember, for example: CollegeBoard, ACT, Florida Shines, Common App, and University Applications.

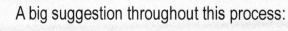

A big suggestion throughout this process:

CREATE A COLLEGE APPLICATION SPECIFIC EMAIL!!

You will receive quite a bit of email from multiple colleges and organizations. Creating a professional-sounding email account is key. Admissions representatives receive emails every day from potential students, so using your FIRST + LAST name is easiest for everyone.

Name/Website	User Name or ID #	Password

HIGH SCHOOL TO COLLEGE ONLINE RESOURCES

✎ All links can be found at www.unmaze.me/links for direct access.

Academic Planning & Research

Name	Description	Website Link
UnMaze.Me	Your Florida College Counseling Website	www.unmaze.me
Job Shadow	Shadow real people's jobs online	http://www.jobshadow.com/
Career One Stop	A source for career exploration, training & jobs	http://www.careeronestop.org/
C'reer App	Matching career paths with colleges	http://www.creer.us/
Career Clusters	Research 16 Career Clusters, and 79 Career Pathways	https://careertech.org/career-clusters
Florida Career Shines	Florida's college and career resources	https://www.floridashines.org
Bureau of Labor Statistics	Find information on duties, education, training, pay, and outlook for hundreds of occupations	https://www.bls.gov/ooh/
CollegeBoard	SAT & College Articles	www.collegeboard.org
ACT	ACT & Resources	www.actstudent.org
NACAC College Fairs	National college fairs with 200+ universities and colleges in attendance	www.gotomyncf.com
College Navigator	Find the right college for you	https://nces.ed.gov/collegenavigator/
College ScoreCard	Compare colleges and financial aid packages	https://collegescorecard.ed.gov/
Cappex	Scholarship & College Search	www.cappex.com
Common Application	An online application for 400+ college and universities throughout the country	www.commonapp.org
Affordable Colleges Online	Distance Learning	http://www.affordablecollegesonline.org/

SCHOLARSHIP & FINANCIAL AID WEBSITES

Name	Description	Website Link
FAFSA	Free Application for Federal Student Aid	https://fafsa.ed.gov/
Bright Futures	Florida state college	http://www.floridastudentfinancialaid.org/ssfad/bf/
Finance Your Future	Provides online courses on financial literacy	http://financeyourfuture.myfloridacfo.com/index.html
Florida College Access Network	State organization to improve college and career readiness	http://www.floridacollegeaccess.org/
CSS Profile	Institutional Financial Aid for certain universities	https://student.collegeboard.org/css-financial-aid-profile
Nest 529	College Savings	https://www.nest529direct.com
Student Loans	Find out about student college loans	https://studentloans.gov
College Reality Check	Education as an Investment	http://collegerealitycheck.com/en/
Student Aid	Federal financial aid planning website	www.studentaid.ed.gov
National Association of Student Financial Aid Administrators	Online calculator to interpret financial aid packages	www.nelliemae.com
Estimated Family Contribution	Calculate your EFC	https://bigfuture.collegeboard.org/pay-for-college/paying-your-share/expected-family-contribution-calculator
Florida FAFSA First Campaign	Find out- Why FAFSA?	http://www.fafsafirst.com/
Raise.Me	Micro-scholarships	www.raise.me
Scholarships.com	Free scholarship search engine	www.scholarships.com
Fastweb	Connection to scholarships, financial aid, and colleges	www.fastweb.com
Scholly app	Personalized scholarship search engine	https://myscholly.com/
FastAid	Free scholarship search	www.fastaid.com

College Planning Calendar

Aug 2017	6	7	8	9	10	11	12
	13	14	15	16	17	18	19
	20	21	22	23	24	25	26 SAT Test Date*
	27	28	29	30	31	1	2
Sep 2017	3	4	5	6	7	8	9
	10	11	12	13	14	15	16
	17	18	19	20	21	22	23
	24	25	26	27	28	29	30
Oct 2017	1 FAFSA Opens	2	3	4	5	6	7 SAT Test Date*
	8	9	10	11	12	13	14
	15	16	17	18	19	20	21
	22	23	24	25	26	27	28
	29	30	31	1 Priority Application Deadline	2	3	4 SAT Test Date*
Nov 2017	5	6	7	8	9	10	11
	12	13	14	15	16	17	18
	19	20	21	22	23	24	25

Dec 2017	3	4	5	6	7	8	9
	10	11	12	13	14	15	16
	17	18	19	20	21	22	23
	24	25	26	27	28	29	30
	31	1	2	3	4	5	6
Jan 2018	7	8	9	10	11	12	13
	14	15	16	17	18	19	20
	21	22	23	24	25	26	27
	28	29	30	31	1	2	3
Feb 2018	4	5	6	7	8	9	10
	11	12	13	14	15	16	17
	18	19	20	21	22	23	24
	25	26	27	28	1	2	3
Mar 2018	4	5	6	7	8	9	10
	11	12	13	14	15	16	17
	18	19	20	21	22	23	24
	25	26	27	28	29	30	31

2018	1	2	3	4	5	6	7
	8	9	10	11	12	13	14
	15	16	17	18	19	20	21
	22	23	24	25	26	27	28
	29	30	1	2	3	4	5
May 2018	6	7	8	9	10	11	12
	13	14	15	16	17	18	19
	20	21	22	23	24	25	26
	27	28	29	30	31	1	2
Jun 2018	3	4	5	6	7	8	9
	10	11	12	13	14	15	16
	17	18	19	20	21	22	23

MAKING THE FINAL DECISION

You have academically prepared, filled out college applications, applied for scholarships and financial aid, received award letters, and now it is time to decide! Many students struggle with that final step of deciding between a few schools. Use this decision-making process sheet to see which school is your "Just Right" school.

Final Choices: _____

Step 1: Review p. 48-50, Finding your "Just Right" College

What were some of the most important attributes you wanted in a college?

Step 2: Review p. 61-63, College Visits Scorecard

Compare the schools in each category by noting strengths and weaknesses of each school.

	School #1	School #2
Academics		
Academic Perks		
Academic Support		
Financial Aid (COA)		
Graduation Track Record		
Outside Opportunities		
Student Life		
Other Considerations		

Step 3: University specific questions

Other questions that should be answered before deciding:

1. HOW ARE MY COLLEGE CREDITS (AICE, IB, DUAL-ENROLLMENT, CERTIFICATES) GOING TO TRANSFER?

2. WHEN AND HOW DO THEY PREPARE ME FOR THE CAREER I WANT? EXAMPLES: INTERNSHIPS, STUDY ABROAD, CAREER CENTERS, RESEARCH OPPORTUNITIES, COLLEGE PARTNERSHIPS

3. WHAT IS THE RETENTION AND PLACEMENT RATE OF THE PROGRAM I WANT?

4. WHAT IS THE PROCESS IF I DECIDE TO CHANGE MAJORS?

5. HOW DID THE OVERALL CULTURE OF THE SCHOOL FEEL TO ME?

6. WHAT ARE SOME ADDITIONAL SCHOLARSHIP POSSIBILITIES?

7. WHICH CAMPUS ACTIVITIES AND RESOURCES WOULD I BE MOST LIKELY TO USE?

8. WHICH COLLEGE WITH THE SCHOLARSHIP AND FINANCIAL AID PACKAGE CAN I AFFORD BOTH IN THE SHORT TERM AND IN THE LONG TERM?

Choosing your "Just Right" college is a big decision. Be sure to talk with your teachers, school counselor, parents, and professionals in your career field to determine what is best for you and your career path.

Your Choice

_____

Thank you for allowing me to be a part of this decision!
I wish you the best for your future.
~Dr. Amanda Sterk~

REFERENCES

Broward State College (n.d.). Career pathways image, Retrieved from https://www.floridacollegesystem.com/students/programs/meta-major_academic_pathways.aspx

CollegeBoard (2011). Four-year graduation rates for four-year colleges. Retrieved from http://media.collegeboard.com/digitalServices/pdf/professionals/four-year-graduation-rates-for-four-year-colleges.pdf

FLDOE (2016), Industry Certifications Earned by Certification- 2008-08 to 2015-16, Retrieved from http://www.fldoe.org/academics/career-adult-edu/research-evaluation/cape-industry-certification.stml

Clinedinst, M., Koranteng, A. & Nicola, T. (2015). State of college admission report. Retrieved from https://www.nacacnet.org/globalassets/documents/publications/research/2015soca.pdf

FCAN (2013). $100 million in Pell Grants left behind: FAFSA completion in Florida. Retrieved from http://www.floridacollegeaccess.org/wp-content/uploads/2013/12/FAFSA-Completion-in-Florida.pdf

Ivory, S. (2016, Sept. 8). NACAC survey: Grades matter most in college admissions. Retrieved from https://www.nacacnet.org/news--publications/newsroom/nacac-survey-grades-matter-most-in-college-admission-/

Miller, T. (2013). Grad rates at public universities in Florida inch higher. Retrieved from http://www.floridacollegeaccess.org/2013/03/13/grad-rates-at-public-universities-in-florida-inch-higher/

PCUF (2016). Private colleges and universities of Florida admission matrix. Retrieved from http://pcuf.net/wp-content/uploads/2014/07/PCUF-guide-2014-pdf.pdf

Powell, F. (2016). Colleges that claim to meet full financial need. Retrieved from https://www.usnews.com/education/best-colleges/paying-for-college/articles/2016-09-19/colleges-that-claim-to-meet-full-financial-need

Schaffer, R. (2017). Kaplan test prep survey: College admissions officers say social media increasingly affects applicants' chances. Retrieved from http://press.kaptest.com/press-releases/kaplan-test-prep-survey-college-admissions-officers-say-social-media-increasingly-affects-applicants-chances

SUS of Florida (2016). 2016 SUS admissions tour MATRIX. Retrieved from http://www.flbog.edu/board/office/asa/admissionstour.php

UF (2013). 2012-2013 Financial aid award. Retrieved from http://www.sfa.ufl.edu/pub/brochures/awardguide1213.pdf

UF (2017). SSAR questions. Retrieved from http://www.admissions.ufl.edu/apply/freshman/ssar-faq

USF (2017). Initial guidelines for freshmen admission, 2016-2017. Retrieved from http://www.usf.edu/admissions/freshman/decisions/index.aspx

ENDORSEMENTS:

College Readiness Experts

"When Dr. Sterk joined FSW's Collegiate High School as a school counselor, our graduating class earned less than $2 million in scholarships. Thanks to Amanda's leadership, knowledge, and programming that figure more than quadrupled in just three short years."

—Larry Miller, Ph.D.,
Dean, School of Education,
Charter Schools, and Dual-Enrollment

"College planning is a multifaceted problem: how do you prepare high school student for the process of not just going to college but making the right choices to get **through** *college cost effectively with a rewarding and gratifying job at the end of the process while at the same time making sure the parents have not bet the farm on the student's decision. Amanda Sterk has dedicated her academic and professional work to solving this student's dilemma.*

Marketing gurus say that cloning oneself assures the message is effectively communicated over and over again. Amanda does that with her College UnMaze Guidebook and her practice. Kudos to Amanda for dedicating herself tirelessly to solving this dilemma.

—Bud Jenkins,
Floridian College Planning Resources, LLC.

"Dr. Sterk is passionate about guiding students through the college process. She continually seeks to collaborate with experts in the field and ensures the highest quality information is passed on to families that need it most. As a college and career counselor, I see how instrumental her College UnMazed Guidebook will be to ALL Florida students."

—Nancy Frede,
Find Your Future Today, Career Coach

"Dr. Sterk has a gifted ability to understand the perspective of others which positions her as a true student advocate. College UnMazed will certainly guide the college applicant in a caring, confident, wise manner.

—Nancy Jordan,
Ed.D. Educator & Administrator

"Amanda is a true asset for parents of high schoolers in our Southwest Florida community. She recognized a need for students to have access to information on navigating the process of obtaining a post-secondary education and has created excellent resources to help guide families."

—Melanie Holaway,
Local Scholarship Expert

Parents

"Amanda is amazing. She truly is filling a need with her site and this guidebook. There is so much information out there and Amanda helps simplify it. She is truly knowledgeable and passionate about what she does. My daughter just finished up with her College UnMazed class in Cape Coral and I couldn't be happier. She has truly opened our eyes! Highly Highly Highly recommend!!!"

—Kathleen, Parent

"This is guidebook is so exciting! You have done wonderful things for our school and now for our community. I am glad that you have written a book to help all high school students and parents out."

—Tracey, Parent

"Amanda not only cares and is passionate about helping students get to college, she also really knows her stuff!"

Julie, Parent

Amanda has played a major role in guiding my eldest daughter through the difficult process of registering for college courses through dual-enrollment, and has also been very influential in guiding our daughter with the different Florida colleges and the many scholarships that are offered.

I can honestly say that Amanda has played a very large part in our daughters' lives this past year. We were very fortunate to find her. She has helped make our move here to the Cape a success and we could have never done this without her!

—Kristie, Parent

Student Testimonials

"You have been such an amazing gift to have! Thank you for allowing me to reach my full potential. Thank you for being an inspiration and motivation in times that I needed it. You are an amazing person. I cannot picture my life going the direction it is going now without you. I admire your love and passion."

—Franklin D.

"Before Dr. Sterk's UnMaze.Me program, I was a fish out of water. My eldest brother had chosen to go into the Navy before applying to a postsecondary institution and this circumstance made me a first-generation college student. While there's a wealth of knowledge at our fingertips with the Internet, nothing compares to the support Dr. Sterk's UnMaze.Me program provided me with tips on how to choose the right school for me based on my "fit," the best ways to fine-tune my personal essay, and how to bargain with colleges for better financial aid packages. I took everything Dr. Sterk taught me and used it in my admissions applications, scholarships, and decision making. I can wholeheartedly and honestly admit that without Dr. Sterk's guidance, I would not have had the courage to push myself out of my comfort zone and aim high."

—Emely R.

ABOUT THE AUTHOR

After being an educator all over the world in places like West Africa, Nicaragua, and throughout the United States, Dr. Amanda Sterk has continued to cultivate her love of travel, writing, and education. Her passion is for guiding families through the educational system so students can reach their full potential.

She lives in Cape Coral, Florida with her husband, two daughters, and two guinea pigs. In Dr. Sterk's free time, she loves to blog, kayak, and travel with her family.

CPSIA information can be obtained
at www.ICGtesting.com
Printed in the USA
BVHW010325180519
548592BV00008B/175/P

CPSIA information can be obtained
at www.ICGtesting.com
Printed in the USA
BVHW010325180519
548592BV00008B/175/P

9 781614 935445